THE MANDELA EFFECT

A HISTORY: THE FIRST DISCOVERIES AND WHAT PEOPLE SAID

FIONA BROOME

NEW FOREST
BOOKS

DEDICATION

This book is gratefully dedicated to Shadowe, to the earliest contributors to Mandela Effect research, and to those who – even now – continue to discover and share their alternate memories (despite risk of being ridiculed).

You've made the Mandela Effect the widespread and accepted phenomenon that it is today. That required courage and independent thinking.

Without a doubt, you've been part of something important, even revolutionary. Its value may seem anecdotal today, but in the future, I think people will look back on this movement as something extraordinary and prescient.

I am truly honored and humbled to have been part of these discoveries, and I thank each and every one of you.

Sincerely,

Fiona Broome

CONTENTS

INTRODUCTION

This is the earliest history of the Mandela Effect – the topic, and what people said when it was first discovered – around 2009 and shortly after that.

I'm Fiona Broome. I created the first Mandela Effect webpage that popularized the phrase.

Looking back at the past fourteen-or-so years, I smile. This has been an unexpected adventure.

At times, it was stressful. I wasn't prepared for the topic's popularity. If I could turn back the clock, I'd handle the deluge of attention very differently.

Nevertheless, I'm grateful for this experience, and the many great people I've met through the websites. We share the same mix of skepticism and a starry-eyed enthusiasm for "what if...?" questions.

Any one of us could have started the Mandela Effect website. I just happened to be in the right place at the right time, with the right background.

For most of my adult life, I've been interested in subjects that other people consider "odd." Most of those topics are related to history or science – or both – in some way.

That's how my past, primary focus – ghost research – led me to other anomalies.

One of those anomalies was the Mandela Effect.

1

OVERVIEW

I thought Nelson Mandela died in prison. I *thought* I remembered it clearly, complete with news clips of his funeral, the mourning in South Africa, some rioting in cities, and the heartfelt speech by his widow.

Then, I found out he was still alive.

My reaction was sensible. "Oh, I must have misunderstood something on the news."

I didn't think about it again for many years, until – in the VIP suite at Dragon Con – "Shadowe," a top member of the event's Security Team, casually mentioned that others *also* "remembered" that Nelson Mandela had died in prison.

That caught my attention in a hurry.

One thing led to another, and – starting in 2009 – my Mandela Effect website connected a large community of people who remembered the same Mandela history as I do.

But that's not all. Others have similar – but different – "false" memories.

Here are a few of the earliest.

Mandela Effect: Billy Graham, too?

One of the earliest conversations was about the death of the Reverend Billy Graham. (Like Mandela, Graham was also alive at the time.)

Some claimed that people were confused, and they'd recalled Graham's *retirement* announcement, or perhaps the televised funeral of Graham's wife.

Those who vividly recall the funeral coverage *strongly* disagree. (Note: The Reverend Billy Graham died in Feb 2018, long after his funeral was discussed on the Mandela Effect website.)

However, *it's not just deaths.*

People have described a variety of odd conflicts between their vivid memories and the world they're currently living in.

The "vanished" Star Trek episode... that never existed

During Dragon Con 2010, a conference attendee insisted that he remembered a Star Trek episode that – according to one of the show's stars – was never even filmed.

The conference guest who remembered the alternate episode wasn't weird or wild-eyed. He was a very normal person, and only referenced the episode as part of a routine conversation.

But then I was there when he heard that the episode never existed. He was stunned and quickly tried to find a logical explanation for his "faulty" memory.

Robert Beltran was part of that conversation because the "alternate" memory involved his character, Chakotay.

(I referenced that – and went into more detail – in my YouTube video about what to do if your memories are "different" from others'.)

However, that was one of several quirky, alternate Star Trek memories that fans and viewers recall.

Berenstein Bears, "Luke, I am your father," and more

Around 2014, when people discovered that there were no "Berenstein Bears" books, and no Star Wars movie included the line, "Luke, I am your father" ... That's when the Mandela Effect went viral.

These aren't simple errors in memory. People recall them clearly, often with astonishing details, exceeding the normal range of forgetfulness.

Even stranger, other people – who don't know each other and often live thousands of miles away – seem to share *identical,* alternate memories.

Later in this book, I'll share a long list of the most popular, shared, alternate memories from the first few years of discoveries.

Next, let's look at how this all started.

2

More Details, and the Website Launch

I may have been the ideal person to popularize the Mandela Effect.

It's not because I think I'm clever, or ever wanted to be famous, or anything like that.

Not at all.

The simple fact is this: I've always been interested in *odd* topics.

Most of them are related to history or science – or both – in some way.

For example, I've spent decades studying ghosts and related anomalies. That's why I've been a regular guest speaker at Dragon Con.

(According to the event's website, "Dragon Con is the largest multimedia, popular culture convention focusing on science fiction & fantasy, gaming, comics, literature, art, music, and film in the universe.")

So, as an invited speaker, I have access to Dragon Con's "green room." (That's a VIP suite where celebrity guests can relax, out of the public eye, between our scheduled panels, etc.

We're an odd group, so green room conversations can be quirky.

The very first Mandela Effect conversation

One day, a few of us were talking about "expanding Earth" theories and related, weird topics. As usual, one anecdote led to another.

At some point, Dragon Con's security manager – called "Shadowe" – said, "That's like the people who remember Nelson Mandela dying many years ago."

Of course, all of us knew that Mandela was still alive, but *I* was one of "those people." I had a clear memory of a televised funeral that – at the time – I'd truly thought marked the passing of Nelson Mandela. (I describe those exact memories at the back of this book.)

After Shadowe's comment, everyone went silent for a minute, and then all of us started talking at once. As it turns out, several of us had mistakenly believed that Mandela had died, but – like me – had dismissed it as simple confusion. (Remember, Mandela was still alive at the time of our conversation.)

At some point, someone – I think it was Shadowe, but it might have been me or someone else – suggested, "let's just call this the Mandela Effect."

So, for the rest of the conversation we used that phrase. After all, it was simpler than repeatedly saying "people who mistakenly recalled Nelson Mandela's death and funeral."

That evening, I went back to my hotel room and spoke with one of my editors. After that, I registered MandelaEffect.com, so we could see how widespread that Mandela memory was, and if anyone had a reasonable explanation for the confusion. (Today, that URL points to my related YouTube channel.)

In my earliest, *very* brief post at that website, I said that I recalled Nelson Mandela's 20th-century death in prison and the funeral that followed it.

Then I opened the website for comment, and told a few friends about my new website.

And so, the Mandela Effect conversations began

Over the following months, several people commented.

Many site visitors lived outside the United States. Most of them were involved in science and technology.

So, the topic became a backdrop for the whimsical, often-geeky conversations that followed.

We weren't entirely serious, but we weren't always joking, either.

As time went on, site visitors suggested *more* "alternate memories"... Major things they recalled that didn't match recorded history.

There wasn't anything firm, adamant, or belligerent about those comments. People were curious and sought answers. That's all.

As a growing community, we tried to debunk some of the alternate memories we had.

Attempted explanations

Usually, we blamed inaccurate newspaper reports.

In an era when newspapers were still enormously popular, competition was fierce. The first newspaper to run with a breaking news story – and feature it as a front-page headline – usually reaped most of the attention... and the highest income for that day.

So, new reporters were often assigned topics *that hadn't happened yet,* but might in the future. That way, senior reporters had content available when they were rushing to meet a deadline.

At times, mistakes were made.

One of the classics was at the close of the 1948 U.S. Presidential election. Some newspapers announced: "Dewey Wins." However, in the morning - after all the votes had been counted - *Truman* was the real winner. Those too-hasty front-page announcements had to be retracted.

Even today, news reporters make mistakes. Or, a pressman might deliberately run a false story, as payback for a salary cut or being given his notice.

After that, the fake story may spread by word-of-mouth before the news agency can retract or correct what they'd said.

Of course, the Internet has magnified the problem. In social media and on websites, fake news has become rampant. Even sites like Snopes can't keep up with the problem.

That's why it was easy for us to believe that our Mandela Effect memories were simple mistakes.

But, some of our "alternate memories" weren't so easy to explain. At times, that was odd enough to be troubling.

So, we joked about them and came up with fantastical explanations, usually involving quantum science, alternative realms, and so on.

It was all lighthearted. Or that's what we told ourselves, anyway.

Soon, more people joined our conversations. They became more serious.

I'm not sure any of us were prepared for the changes ahead.

3

— • —

THEN, THEORIES - AND CONFLICTS - BEGAN

B y 2012, fresh reports of *new* alternate memories were flooding in.

Also, some people took the topic *very* seriously. They didn't seem to understand our previous, flippant speculation.

Others – thankfully, just a few – overlooked everyday errors and clickbait, took tabloid news seriously, or accepted rumors at face value.

A few had an axe to grind, or they'd already decided that a cover-up or conspiracy was involved.

They were in sharp contrast to the rest of us who attributed most – *not all* – Mandela Effects to simple mistakes, mental health issues, spoofs and parodies.

We knew we had unexplained memories. Things that didn't match recorded history.

And, we still mused about scientific (and pseudo-scientific) explanations that verged on fantasy and science fiction.

For example, we speculated that we might be in a holodeck, similar to one on "Star Trek." Or, we might be experiencing time slips or brushes with parallel realities.

But increasingly, visitors wanted to talk about *specific memories* rather than the fun, broader, "what if?" questions that had sparked early interest.

I was okay with that because so many people seemed to find comfort in reading others' reports of similar or identical alternate memories.

With the assurances that they were not alone, they seemed happy to go back to their everyday lives. If they had a few lingering questions about their memories, that seemed okay.

Then, more scientists chimed in, and Mandela Effect conversations diverged even more.

(Of course, since I've never met most of these people in real life, I couldn't confirm who they were, or verify their backgrounds. Were they actual scientists? I have no idea.)

Regardless of their credentials, the ideas they suggested were intriguing. Some were downright fascinating to those of us who identify as geeks and nerds.

However, our conversations' general good humor was fading, perhaps faster than we realized at the time.

The CERN connection

Several visitors speculated about a link between the Mandela Effect and research at CERN and particle accelerators.

Others wanted to talk about repeating patterns in the Mandela Effect reports, and related "markers." For me, those were the most interesting conversations, though – of course – I took many of them with a grain of salt.

However, some comments came from jokers, pranksters, and trolls, and many seem to have agendas that made no sense to me. Worse, moderating those comments took several hours a day.

Some visitors did not seem to understand that – for me – the website was a hobby. Oh, it was a *fascinating* hobby, but I still had a "day job" as a paranormal researcher, author, and journalist.

This is probably a good point for me to explain that I already have a full-time career.

My day job

Beginning in the mid-to late 1990s, I created – and, as of 2023, still maintain – HollowHill.com, one of the Internet's largest, free, ghost hunting resources.

At one point, it was home to over 500 articles I'd written about ghosts and haunted places.

Then, once TV shows – such as "Ghost Hunters" – popularized the topic, publishers and TV shows hired me to work with them. I debunked the fake hauntings. I found little-known locations that seem to have credible ghost reports. And, I explained how to investigate ghost stories from both practical and historical viewpoints.

I've written about things such as the Marfa Lights in Texas, flying snakes (also in Texas), the *real* hound of the Baskervilles, and whether Mrs. O'Leary's cow actually started the famous Chicago fire.

But, mostly I write about ghosts and ghost hunting. That's what brought me to the attention of science fiction and fantasy conventions such as Dragon Con.

I believe that ghosts are real. After all, it's difficult for me to think that Deity would prevent people from returning to visit their homes and families after passing on.

Also, in a scientific context, there's the Law of Energy Conservation.

So, whether you call it a soul or something else, the energy or life spirit continues, in a different form.

That's why I take most – not all – reports of ghostly spirits very seriously.

- If someone is delighted that they once encountered a ghost, I listen to the story and congratulate them.

- If they're terrified because they've been awoken by an "old hag" who held them down in bed, I advise them that it's not ghostly or demonic. In fact, many people will have that kind of experience – known as sleep paralysis – up to three times during their lives. It's odd but not necessarily dangerous.

Note: Whether all "haunted" sites have ghosts... That's another matter. It's why I wrote a book called "Is Your House Haunted?" (Most "haunted" homes have electrical, plumbing, structural, or other environmental issues, so they merely *seem* haunted.)

How this affects my view of the Mandela Effect

When I moderated comments at the Mandela Effect website – I followed similar guidelines.

- If the person seemed to be excited that they might have had a Mandela Effect experience, I was happy to agree with them.

- If the person seemed anxious or upset – especially if they felt victimized by some conspiracy, or as if they were losing their minds – I did my best to suggest reasonable alternative explanations. (I also made a YouTube video about this, called "Trust Your Memories.")

In my opinion, they're all – technically – paranormal experiences. And, since I wasn't there at the time, I'm not equipped to evaluate what actually happened.

Maybe their experience can be explained in normal terms. Maybe it can't.

From my point of view, it was most important to calm those who are panicking, and gather data while cheerfully listening to those celebrating their unusual experiences.

But nothing prepared me for what was about to happen to the Mandela Effect.

4

FACT-CHECKING, GEORGE TAKEI, AND A DILEMMA

As more people learned about the Mandela Effect, they seemed to affirm each other's memories.

Being naturally skeptical, I worried about this. The Internet's "wow, that's just like me!" effect can spiral in unhealthy ways.

If the site's comments became little more than an echo chamber, I couldn't determine the scope, breadth, and *actual* frequency of the Mandela Effect.

That's why I created a post where people could report their alternate memories, *but site visitors would not see what that person had reported.*

Then, I waited to see if any hidden comments at *that* post reflected similar alternate memories, and if there were any *patterns* among them.

It wasn't the most scientific of tests, but I saw a surprising number of correlated reports.

It's possible that, in some cases, the original poster returned to the Mandela Effect website. Then, using a different username and a spoofed IP number, they hoped the second (or third, or fourth) report might convince me it was a *legitimate* alternate memory.

However, I also watched for consistent typos, speech patterns, and so on.

Most – but not *all* – of those reports seemed credible.

I wondered: Should we be taking the Mandela Effect more seriously?

That's when I briefly created a private forum for a few Mandela Effect "old timers." There, in private conversations, some of us began saying, "Wait, maybe this *is* real."

It's not that I had thought people were just "making things up." It's not that I defaulted to ideas of confabulation or conspiracy theories, either.

Mostly, I didn't know what to think about all of this, particularly since I still had no reasonable explanation for my *own* memories of Mandela's 20th century funeral.

That's when visitors to the more public Mandela Effect website started offering serious theories about what was going on.

Some were based in scientific speculation. Others were grounded in statistical analyses. And yes, a few were silly, but couldn't be wholly dismissed.

After all, though we couldn't seem to agree on very much, we were still having fun speculating.

Maybe it was the weirdness of those conversations. Maybe it was the flippant humor, and our continuing "what if?" discussions, chasing down every possible explanation or pattern of reports.

Or maybe it was just comforting for people to find others who shared their "odd" memories.

Either way, traffic to the Mandela Effect site was approaching critical mass. I could barely keep up with the comments, and my career was faltering. I'd turned down multiple TV shows, but I still had publishers awaiting books, and my own websites to maintain.

The day George Takei changed everything

Around 2014, the dam broke.

It started when George Takei posted in social media about his memories of the *Berenstein* Bears.

Like many people, he remembered them as *Berenstein Bears* not *Berenstain Bears.*

Since the Mandela Effect website already *had* an article about that topic, my website was at the top of the list when someone searched Google for Berenstein Bears.

(Several websites, including "Above Top Secret," discussed alternate memories, even prior to the launch of the Mandela Effect website. However, my site was the one with the most Berenstain/Berenstein content.)

That was the tipping point.

Suddenly, tens of thousands – and then *hundreds* of thousands – of visitors came to the Mandela Effect website, steadily. Many had a lot to say on multiple topics.

What had been a hobby website, now demanded both bandwidth and considerable, daily attention.

I wasn't prepared for either of those.

And then I made mistakes

I moved the site to a better hosting plan, believing the Berenstein Bears flurry would soon subside.

I was wrong.

It didn't. In fact, the traffic kept soaring, and – with it – snarky comments and unabashed trolls.

And meanwhile, moderating *all* of the comments, I was working myself to exhaustion.

That's not an excuse for using poor judgment as a moderator, or for sometimes being rude with my replies.

At that time, about 25% of comments referenced conspiracies and psyops themes.

They didn't – and still don't – interest me.

Also, despite dramatically increasing hosting bills, *I'd never considered monetizing the Mandela Effect website.*

So, as friends, fans, and visitors complained when the site crashed daily, over and over again, I tried some advertising on the site.

I *hated* how it looked, and quickly removed it.

Then I created unique T-shirts with Mandela Effect graphics, hoping to offset the hosting bills. A few T-shirts sold – less than a dozen – but those efforts seemed to spark outrage. Some claimed that I was only "in it for the money."

That's when I stopped approving snarky, weird, and off-topic comments, and let the site crash from time to time.

I did make one exception: I approved a *very* odd comment by someone calling himself Mr. Stain. To this day, I cannot explain why his comment intrigued me, but it did. It also got the attention of several longtime visitors to the Mandela Effect website.

What "Mr. Stain" said:

23 July 15 at 5:04 am

This has nothing to do with financial gain the A is a marker for every time processor in the event of an emergency to understand what reality they are in, there are so many more markers that are hidden from the public yet each letter stands for age, date, time and sequence. This information is true and has been provided for your understanding by a fellow time processor...please watch out for 2029! Be prepared and watch out for the awakening, this is not make sense now but will soon and please stop using your cell phones they are the key ingredient of your societies collapse.

I was intrigued by his reference to markers, and I wondered if his spelling, "prepared," was deliberate, or just aligned with other apparent typos in his comment. Most likely, English wasn't his first language. (Or, perhaps he deliberately made it look that way.)

Another user – choosing a name similar to "John Dean" – contributed equally fascinating and sometimes cryptic references. They made sense, sometimes in a non-sequitur way.

In addition, his username – and his (their?) phrasing – reminded me of a *different* John Dean, from the Watergate era.

Out of curiosity, I checked the IP number associated with the new person's comment. Its location added credibility. That still intrigues me, though that's all I'm willing to say, to protect that person's privacy.

Readers replied, making anomalous, unexpected references to those signs. The surge of interest and the sense of authenticity – even familiarity – in what they said... It was startling, in a way.

It's difficult for me to articulate any logical continuity to them. (In a way, I want to say "sense of direction," instead of "continuity." Words don't seem adequate here; long-time Mandela Effect followers will understand that.) I still can't, though I've often mused about the frequent use of those Chevron signs as landmarks. (Why them, and not other gas stations' signs? Or McDonald's or Burger King signs, and so on?)

At that point, I began to realize that I was out of my depth as a webmaster, comment moderator, and perhaps even as a researcher.

Changes were necessary.

5

THE END OF THE MANDELA EFFECT WEBSITE?

As much as the hosting issues, trolls, and volume of comments had eroded my enthusiasm for the Mandela Effect, comments like Mr. Stain's – as well as replies to them – had re-energized me.

In addition, discussions about "markers" – things that seemed to mark when or where a Mandela Effect event might occur or be recalled – took our online conversations in a new direction.

Suddenly, more people who sounded scientific, as well as a few who claimed a CERN connection, weighed in with some extraordinary ideas.

With them, I *also* saw an increase in private messages warning me that the Mandela Effect website posed a problem related to an experiment, or perhaps *several* experiments.

I ignored those warnings.

I still don't know what they meant.

At that point, I wondered if the Mandela Effect website was just one of many involved in this kind of speculation.

Was the genie out of the lamp?

DDoS attacks followed. Bandwidth usage went through the roof. Comments became increasingly strange, or perhaps it just *seemed* that way because I was exhausted.

At the same time, the ghost hunting fad fell off a virtual cliff. Many of the most enduring ghost hunting TV series were canceled, or became absurdly extreme to maintain ratings. In addition, my related books weren't selling, and many of them contain outdated information anyway.

I took a couple of weeks off, to regain my perspective.

I had to tell my publisher that there might never be a Mandela Effect book. If there was any *credible* pattern to the reports, I had neither the time nor energy to analyze those patterns.

In addition, it seemed to me then – and it still does – that most Mandela Effect enthusiasts are interested in active discussions. Other websites and forums such as Reddit are better equipped for those conversations.

I closed the Mandela Effect website to new comments, and asked people to e-mail me instead.

That was *not* one of my better ideas.

By the middle of 2017, when bandwidth issues were a problem (yet again), I was receiving 5000 to 6000 non-spam e-mails – *per day* – via the Mandela Effect website. I didn't have time to read them, much less reply.

I felt *so* guilty, I had to take action.

So, I removed the contact page, as well.

In the silence that followed, I had time to look back over the history of the Mandela Effect website.

I realized that the site had long outgrown its initial goal. Worse, I'd never had a business plan for it, or an exit strategy. Others have effectively monetized the topic, but I guess my brain isn't wired that way.

At that point, as a hobby, the Mandela Effect had kind of taken over my life, and with my tacit permission.

Oh, for a long time, it was tremendous fun. I met *wonderful* people through comments and e-mails.

Looking back on it now, I think the Mandela Effect website has been one of the most fun things I've ever been part of.*

Yes, it's easy for me to dwell on the not-so-fun aspects. Despite that, the conversations at the site – in the early days, anyway – were at least 90% entertaining.

Would I restart the site as a gathering place for Mandela Effect conversations?

Maybe, but probably not.

As I'm writing this, I'm adding video content to my related YouTube channel. Conversations can resume there, moderated (at least lightly) by YouTube.

I'll see what happens. That may be a fun project, or - after giving it a test-drive - I may look in the mirror and sternly tell myself to walk away.

*My most fun experiences...? My years in California, being part of Bjo Trimble's original team, putting together the very first Star Trek conventions. I recall setting up chairs in the big lecture halls, taping down electrical cords with Jimmy Doohan ("Scotty") and Bill

Campbell ("Squire of Gothos"), and helping Grace Lee Whitney ("Yeoman Janice Rand") at her dealers'-room table's guests.

Those are great memories.

So, yes, I *did* know George Takei from those conventions, though I'm sure he didn't (and still doesn't) recall that, when he posted about the Berenstein/Berenstain Bears.

I look back on that coincidence and chuckle. It really *is* a small world!

6

————— ✦ —————

LOOKING BACK, LOOKING FORWARD

The phrase "Mandela Effect" began as part of a weird, wonderful conversation at Dragon Con.

Now, it's so widely known, mainstream media reference it every week. From Scientific American to Good Housekeeping magazine, and from CNN to the Today Show, it seems as if everyone has an opinion.

Even better, most people have a few Mandela Effect memories of their own.

Seeing how this topic has spread, I smile. There were some challenges and more than a few frustrations, but – in general – being part of the Mandela Effect's discovery and expansion has been great fun.

I'm not sure where Mandela Effect studies go from here, but I can hardly wait to see how science (finally?) explains this... if they ever do.

Mostly, I'm honored and humbled to have been part of this adventure with you.

Thank you!

In the next sections of this book, you'll see how our online conversations began, and how other topics entered our conversations.

It's been a wild journey, with lots of zany theories – and bizarre memories – shared, especially in those early days.

Some will make you smile, others will make you chuckle and perhaps shake your head in disbelief.

However, some of those comments may make you pause and say, "Wait. I remembered that, too!"

ORIGINAL COMMENTS - PART 1

These are samples of the comments left at the very first, original, Mandela Effect article... The one where I talked about my strange memories of Mandela's death, and asked if others had similar memories. (Obviously, they did, and not just about Mandela.)

However, the software sometimes saved those comments *very much* out-of-sequence. So, note the dates as you read them. (And I apologize for any weird formatting. There's a LOT of content here, and – editing-out one-line "me, too" comments seemed to skew line breaks, and so on. Well, hey, it's the Mandela Effect topic, and – around that – all *kinds* of weird things seem happen.)

The Comments... *not* just about Nelson Mandela

Perry Ware says:

10 April 11 at 2:05 pm

Both my wife and I remember Nelson Mandela dying in prison. Included in this memory are the funeral snippets on TV and a legal flap over book rights involving his Widow. We also remember that David Soul of the 70's show Starsky and Hutch comiting suicide on or near christmas because he was dispondant over his wife's cancer!

Even news reports of relatives and police discovering his body underneath the christmas tree. You can imagine myself and my wife's reaction when we saw David Soul make an appearance as a cameo on the remake of Starsky and Hutch movie. We sat in silence and stunned by the revelation that Mr. Soul was indeed alive. Do you feel that these so called false memories just might be a shadow effect or "bleed through" of events in a parallel universe?

Fiona says:

12 April 11 at 8:27 am

Perry,

Thanks for your comments.

I think the shadow or "bleed through" effect is possible. The possibility of a "Sliders" effect is also likely, as is Fred Alan Wolf's speculation about experiences when we seem to be asleep.

In addition, I'm hearing more descriptions of extremely vivid dreams... experiences so real, people have difficulty believing they didn't actually happen. (At the same time, these people know they occurred during sleep, and that baffles them.)

I believe that something is going on, and whatever it is, it's increasing: More people, more vivid (and baffling) memories, and more people talking about this.

Like you, I recall the legal flap over the book rights — and commercial rights, in general — after Nelson Mandela's death. However, at that point I was fairly bored with the amount of press coverage after the funeral, so I didn't pay much attention to the details. I just remember it happening.

I'm not sure what's happening, but the evidence is growing: We seem to be crossing time streams and realities. I have no idea what this means, but I'm fascinated by it!

Sincerely,

Fiona

Robert Crowder says:

1 September 13 at 12:07 pm

I was in High school in the mid 80s and I remember that we discussed Mandelas Death in my Geography and economics classes

bob says:

7 June 15 at 9:23 pm

I could not remember the time period, but do remember my Dad and I watching the evening news when it was reporting on Mandela's death. I remember it because I remember my Dad's opinion of him, that he was not a great man, but a communist. My Dad kept up on things.

Robert Crowder says:

30 June 15 at 3:39 pm

I haven't thought about this in a while , but last week I was going through some boxes @ my Dads home and found some of my old notebooks and it contains a copy of the current event that I turned in the week ending on March 11 , 1983 . My report was only detailed about his death in prison and that he had been sick for a while . It focused on how the country of South Africa was pulled together due to his passing . I did not write the Actual date of his death , but I assume it was earlier that week . We had to turn a current event summary in Every Friday about something that happened that week for my Economics class . I am scanning a copy to my Hard drive but do not see a way to post it here . I did not receive a grade on the paper , just a check at the top of the page to remark that I had done my work . Although I have this paper in hand , It is disturbing to me that what I remember is True . I am kinda Freaked over it . My Dad does not remember it but is confused as to why it exists as he knows I could not have recently planted it there .

Vivek narain says:

1 July 15 at 8:56 am

Some where in this site,a year or so back, I had quoted '83 death,but later I found that the particular year was never mentio ned.Now that the '83 appears, was it an intrigue within an intrigue or '83 has been mentioned at least a few times ? since it was not my memory but I had only quoted, please verify.

Fiona Broome says:

1 July 15 at 9:13 am

Vivek, I'm seeing 1983 mentioned several times in 2012 comments by others. I'm still looking for your comment with that date, but it may have been lost in one of the server reboots, where they restored the site from backups. Unfortunately, some comments were perma- nently lost. (I backup the site about once every 10 days, but, alas, if our hosting service has another issue — probably more a "when" than an "if" — it's always possible that some comments will be lost.)

Wonderbread says:

1 October 15 at 1:56 pm

I too have weird memories around Nelson Mandela's death. I was very, very little at the time, and the only way I "remembered" this was the "trigger" from others saying, he's still alive and he died only recently. I also distinctly remember the Berenstein bears as being stein not stain. Distinctly. I wonder what would happen if we could alter time lines? Would we be able to bring back deceased loved ones? I'm fascinated by all of this. Thank you for sharing and Thank you Ken Dolan for mentioning your paper and actually finding something you wrote back in the 80's. Must be a super spooky feeling. I don't know what I'd do if I had that paper. I'm sure this Nelson Mandela thing goes deeper than we even know, but what if they realized there would be instability unless they "resurrected" Nelson Mandela, and they did it through a "clone" or someone who looked a lot like him. Using them instead, hoping people wouldn't remember his death. Just a guess.

Danielle says:

15 August 15 at 3:49 am

I was in grade 4 in 1997 when I learned nelson Mandela was dead. It was black history month.

My confusion later in life when I heard about him in the news, I was baffled that I believed for so long and so surely he already died.

Bryan says:

24 August 15 at 2:41 am

The same exact thing happened to me! It was black history month in middle school several of my classmates covered Mandela however one even brought in old laminated news clippings that their parents had saved, I was able to read these with my own two eyes...

Lauren Alise says:

27 August 15 at 9:52 pm

I am the same age as you and I also remember learning about his death in school. 100%. certain.

James says:

14 October 13 at 12:43 pm

How do you guys know your consciousness wasn't transferred to this dimension at some point... If that were so, it appears to me that you all ended up in the wrong one! Got the raw end of some cosmic event perhaps, or some meddling by other dimensional entities? Or are you of the opinion that it could more possibly be a natural occurence? Perhaps the folds between dimensions connect at some point?

Seriously now, this all sounds like pretty odd stuff. Stranger things are true I guess. I came here with the mind to ridicule you because of the page title, but after I finished reading the intro and some of these comments, I realised I was quite interested. How long ago are we talking here – about these memories? 30 years ago? Do any of these memmories connect in time somehow? Could it have been a propaganda piece you witnessed? Or perhaps Nelson was swapped with a clone or lookalike before he made his return. ... again, weirder things are true – but somebody would have realised unless our brainwaves are controlled – which sounds like a tinfoil hat theory. Sometimes this kind of stuff tears away the foundatations of my thinking if I entertain it. And that would mean nothing I know can be relied up – which is no fun. Will I have to wait until you've written your book before I can learn what's of value here?

Sincerely, James

Fiona Broome says:

14 October 13 at 2:43 pm

James,

My best bet is that it's something involving parallel realities and "sliding" between them. And, at this point, the book isn't even close to being completed, because I'm not confident about any answers we've thought of. We're guessing. That's all.

I'm trying to make time (no pun intended) to sort the threads into main topics — Mandela, Billy Graham, Neil Armstrong, etc. — but this has to be a spare-time project, for now.

My guess is that this happens to almost everyone, but only a small percentage of people say, "Wait a minute...," and can't accept that they "misremembered" or "forgot" or something facile like that. (And, only a small percentage of those people find this website and leave comments.)

I don't think this phenomenon is terribly unusual, but since it breaks the timeline rules the way most people (comfortably) like to think of them, it's easier for most people to find a variation of denial that works, rather than think that there was a fold in dimensions, or a slide, or whatever variation of that makes the most sense to the individual.

Cheerfully,

Fiona

bob says:

7 June 15 at 9:28 pm

What would seem pertinent is this: sometime since the late 1980s, Russia, the U.S., or somebody discovered and developed some kind of technology involving time travel. It might only be time travel for information. A physicist once joked to a reporter, after his group had succeeded in making cesium atoms travel faster than light, "Of course, this doesn't mean we can send information to the past. " If the government could send information to the past, it could prevent every terrorist attack, win any battle or war, and manipulate the economy for a long time without a collapse.

Fiona Broome says:

8 June 15 at 7:57 am

bob, thanks! That's great speculation. I think many of us have wondered about this kind of issue, in general, and it's interesting to think about in terms of the Mandela Effect.

judith says:

3 June 14 at 1:28 pm

I want to know if anyone else who remembers these things had a near death experience in the late 80 or early 90. maybe we died and passed into an alternate reality......

but I too remember Billy graham and Mandela. I thought David soul also was gone by suicide in the 80?s......

I thought I was alone in this. can anyone figure this out?

Li says:

12 July 13 at 12:40 pm

Are you sure you're not getting David Soul mixed up with Pete Duel?

Perry Ware says:

7 December 13 at 1:26 pm

I am a theatre instructor and director in California and have considered David Soul to be (have been) a much underrated actor. When he died I showed film clippings of his work in the teleplay of Stephen King's "Salem's Lot" My students agreed that it was a shame that Mr. Soul had passed. I have asked former students if they remember the 30 minute unit on David Soul's acting ability, and of course they don't.

Fiona Broome says:

7 December 13 at 1:29 pm

Mr. Ware... wow. That's an amazing, very credible first-person account of a memory connected to David Soul's death. Thank you!

Pol says:

6 December 13 at 1:54 am

I read a lot of sites about this sort of thing also along with conspiracy theories and other related subjects, but never leave comments.

I have a lot of my own theories to what is going on and yes some people would probably think me mad.

But today is 6/12/2013 The morning after the announcement of Nelson Mandela's death. he was also announced as dead on the 26/6/2013. I also recall something about him dying in prison in the 80s, But the logical part of my brain is telling me this must have been something to do with the end/death of an era. But there is something at the back of my mind telling me the story, Nelson Mandela never got to reside in the bungalow built for him on robbyn Island because he died before he got to leave his cell ? this Is a vivid memory. I also recall my surprise a year or so later when a news story went out about him and how living alone in the bungalow will soon becoming to an end when Nelson Mandela is released.

Also as a child I recall going to see billy graham with my mother, at a local festival. I live in a small uk town, not really a high profile place for such a visit, but he came and I was there. yet when I mention it to people no one else seems to know about it, I also recall his death years ago.

I also have recall of dreams ?? or are they dreams ?? they are so vivid that years on I recall them scene by scene. one particular one was so real and would have been news worthy. immediately after the dream I looked in all the papers to see if it had been reported on, this took place in the very early 80s,, I never found anything about the event back then, but my dream was reported on in the 90s as an actual event, and it unfolded before my eyes again.

Fiona Broome says:

6 December 13 at 7:18 am

Pol, thank you for your comments.

I maintain that the rich context of these memories distinguish them from mere "oh, I must have misunderstood something I heard on the news," and so on.

However, the dream issue is interesting. I've been intrigued by Dr. Fred Alan Wolf's speculation in the quantum field, and dreams may be an access point to parallel realities.

And, like you, I wonder if this is a marker of some kind. It's as if it's a formal recognition that things have shifted.

Sincerely,

Fiona

Denise says:

5 December 13 at 10:38 pm

I also remember he died before as well, there are many other also such as Dick Clark I now remember he died twice, it keeps happening more frequent, and I don't have alsheimers either. My husband rented a new movie that was just released, but I had all ready seen a few years ago, he didn't believe me at first, I said pause it, I will tell you what happens. I was right, I had seen it before, but how could I have seen it before when it was just released. Timeline shifts happening alot if people are noticing it.

Fiona Broome says:

6 December 13 at 7:29 am

Denise,

Thanks for the comment. I really appreciate people mentioning other moments that fit this pattern. I think you're the first to mention Dick Clark.

Your experience with the movie and your husband is excellent. It's important that others close to us realize that we're not "confused," so we have someone to talk with about our alternate memories, and we're believed.

Sincerely,

Fiona

Travis says:

11 August 15 at 5:05 pm

The Berenstein Bears thing really stuck out to me I know it was stein because my mom use to grill me for not spelling it right. Also we would have pronounced it stain not sine like. I am only 22 now but I distinctly remember learning in school that Mandela had passed away in prison in the 80s. To the woman talking about a movie and knowing what was happening had the exact same moment in the pirates of the Caribbean movie during the first one when they blow up the ship I "predicted" or felt like I had seen the entire next 30 mintue scene before it had happened the opening day of the movie. How could that be possible?

Jon says:

6 December 13 at 9:09 am

Hmmm very intriguing. Kind of reminds me of the episode "The road not taken" in the 1st season of "Fringe." I can't say for sure if I've experienced such a phenomenon myself, but I recall an incident when I was a young teen in high school about a song that became an international hit. Umm trying to recall it with 100% cerainty just now is difficult, but I think it might've been Roxette's "The Look"? What I remember though was that to me this song was not new and so I felt like I was experiencing some sort of deja vu! I was so adamant I recall telling my sister it has to be a remix as I was so sure I'd heard this song in the past. Finally I came to the conclusion that I must've dreamed about it or had a premonition years before.

Another incident I recall–which I've since learned has a logical explanation to it and I only relate as an example–centers on Spielberg's flick "The Goonies." I went to see this movie at the cinema as a youngster and vividly recalled a scene involving an octopus below the pirate ship. However, when I saw this movie on TV years later this scene was not shown. I started to doubt myself and thought that I must've dreamed this entire sequence in my head. But, how could I or why would I?! Later in the early 2000s I discovered via the internet that others remembered this scene too in spite of it not being shown on TV or included in the VHS version of the movie. So I wasn't delusional after all! I finally was able to watch this scene again for the first time in about 20 years a few years ago now after my sister bought it on DVD for her daughters to watch. The aforementioned scene was included in the deleted scenes section!

John says:

20 June 14 at 10:39 am

Holy crap I remembered the octopus scene as well when I read what you wrote... thankful that I stuck it out because that is legit creepy if it didn't exist!

Steve says:

14 August 15 at 5:35 pm

That thing about the movie happened to my when I was 3 or 4. My uncle just bought pink Floyd the wall and ask me and my mom to watch it with him I saw the first few minutes and wanted to play or something. And I told my my mom I already saw this movie the told me I didn't and I replied " this is the movie where the boy throws the dead rat in the river. That's all i remembered still odd.

judith says:

3 June 14 at 1:22 pm

I too remember david soul committing suicide in the 80's........all this is just too weird

Glenda says:

28 May 15 at 10:28 pm

I believe they have been cloned

A W1Z4RD 22 says:

25 August 15 at 4:09 am

your thoughts are not in vain.

if they can 3d print organs publicly now (which they can) anything is possible

RyanKW says:

13 August 15 at 11:31 am

I posted the David Soul thing to my friend who's older than I. Her response:

"It was Michael Galser's wife that had cancer, not David Souls."

Hope this helps.

wb says:

19 August 15 at 5:19 pm

De Ja Vu and retroactive memories (where your brain sort of "fills in" a previous memory with some more recent knowledge, making you think that you had that info from the beginning) are other phenomenons to explain this type of thing, aren't they? Just haven't seen them discussed much

Fiona Broome says:

20 August 15 at 9:12 am

wb, yes, I believe there's some overlap in those concepts.

Brian says:

15 September 15 at 7:39 am

I remember reading a bio on Bjo Trimble (Of Star Trek fandom) who spoke of David Soul in the past tense. I didnt give it much thought until I read your post.....

Celi says:

23 October 15 at 12:21 pm

Hi, I thought I was alone in this until just a few minutes ago while watching a video on youtube. The day I heard that Nelson Mandela died on the news I was next to my parents and I was like "...but he died a long time ago" they told me no he just died and I said "He died in prison a long time ago" and they said that I had my thoughts crossed with someone else but because I saw it on the news I kept trying to think who was I confusing him with. After all that which was maybe a 20 minute thought process for me I just let it go and said to myself if it's on the news now then I guess I'm wrong.

I just heard about the Mandela Effect the funny thing is that I remember a lot of things that are way off but I just kept thinking something was off about me. I now feel a little strange about finding this out but in a way kind of makes me feel better but still in a bit of disbelieve.

Scott says:

11 April 11 at 6:55 pm

Clear distinct memory of the Nelson Mandela funeral on tv in the early 80's

Diana says:

11 February 14 at 2:39 am

I remember David Soul dying, and I've never heard of Pete Duel.

maddie says:

2 March 14 at 11:54 am

same here i have never heard pf peter duel but i have thought for years david soul was dead after hearing a news report that he had committed suicide, only just found out by reading this he did not.

Lani says:

12 April 11 at 4:37 pm

I had a similar experience but it was regarding the birth of Freddi Prince Jr and Sarah Michelle Gellar's child... I'm positive that I saw it mentioned on the news back in 2003-04 that they were expecting... It was either the longest pregnancy in history or something similar to the above events... Also, I've had a crush on Freddi Prince Jr since I was about nine... So it would have been something I was paying attention to...

Tam says:

21 August 13 at 4:45 am

I also remember them expecting

Tamara Thorne says:

13 April 11 at 4:41 pm

I don't have any recollections about Mandela, but do have pretty clear memories of Billy Graham's death. And, as Lani above says, the Gellar-Prince child. I thought that happened years ago, too.

Fiona says:

13 April 11 at 5:12 pm

Hi Tamara,

The Billy Graham memory seems to really rattle people. It's a relatively recent memory, and so it's still pretty clear in people's minds. When they find out he's still alive, they sometimes turn introspective in a blink. It's like they start wondering what else isn't true in their memories.

Really, I sometimes feel guilty for even mentioning the Billy Graham memory. People can get really upset.

The Gellar-Prince child sounds like a really good one to study. I'm always interested in stories like that because they're so distinct. It's not that someone's gone — like the Graham and Mandela memories — but something less easily dismissed as a mixed-up memory.

Thanks for commenting!

Cheerfully,

Fiona

Brian says:

15 September 15 at 7:49 am

I have a thought/ theory. Have you ever tried a poll about whoever has had these shifts might also be autistic/ Aspergers to a degree or more? I have Aspergers, and well, my shifts are like a car with a bad transmission- jarring and disorienting.

C.A. Low says:

13 April 11 at 4:38 pm

I have experienced this many times. Not only Mandela's death, but also the death of Muammar Gaddafi several years ago, events in the lives of friends that they do not recall, and the movement or disappearance of landmarks/buildings. I lived across the street from a mother daughter for 2 years, but recently was told she had no daughter and never had. I believe this phenomena to be related to track-timeline shifts in which something occurs that changes a time line, perhaps something significant past/future on a parallel line. I believe that the persons who 'remembers' what has been changed do so because they were engaged/invested in it a meaningful way. If that engagement was not present, then only the current reality will be remembered.

Fiona says:

13 April 11 at 5:02 pm

C. A.,

That's a really interesting idea about engagement and how it affects reality & memories.

I'm reminded of a friend's very startling 'Mandela Effect' moment: He was using the Google maps feature that allows you to see street views, and he was virtually strolling down his own 'Memory Lane'. However, when he went to look at the elementary school he'd attended — a fairly modern building at the time — the building on the site is Victorian.

While it's possible that Google got it wrong, or the Victorian building was moved to the site after this friend's school was torn down... well, those seem unlikely after he double-checked the location.

And really, nobody is likely to 'forget' the school they went to as a child.

However, he wouldn't have known about this alternate memory if he hadn't actually looked for his school on Google Maps.

So, it makes me wonder how many other reality shifts some of us might find, if we started looking. As it is, we only seem to notice the ones that are placed in front of us — for example, news headlines that don't fit the context of our memories.

As Alice in Wonderland said, 'Curiouser and curiouser!'

Cheerfully,

Fiona

Laura says:

9 July 12 at 1:57 am

As soon as I read what you said about previously remembering Gaddafis death I started gagging. This is really strange, I am not an emotional person but I am sitting here and my eyes are welling up. What is this? I remember this. Footage of a runway and a white plane. Omg.

randi says:

18 January 13 at 3:41 am

same here. im covered in goosebumps.

Peaches says:

24 March 14 at 9:08 am

I remember Ghadafi's death as well. I am sitting at the office thinking "Hold up... I recall he died before".

Kelsey says:

13 August 15 at 3:26 pm

Same here. My eyes are welling and I have chills.

Dan B says:

24 December 13 at 2:55 am

Surprisingly, I also remember Sarah Michelle Gellar being pregnant right before Scooby Doo 2 was to premiere.

I've been getting the oddest deja vu moments throughout 2013. Some very personal. Where I'll tell a friend, "You said this and this and that." And said friend will stare at me blankly. I've never struggled to separate so-called reality from fiction until this year. I'm a writer so that boundary has never been blurred. But these days it is. Roommates of mine report me screaming in my nightmares, laughing maniacally or whimpering. And I repeat: this has never happened to me before. I'm a well-adjusted, fun-loving, tertiary educated adult with many close friends. It does feel as if something wrong is happening to my sense of perception though... Perhaps as another thought: have you heard of the Earth 1 and Earth 2 scenario following the 21 December 2012 mass ascension plot? Basically gaia (the earth) entered a cross-dimensional portal meant to separate the minds ready for 5-dimensional existence and those who want to be stuck in 3D (Earth 2). It seems like this fracture is still happening en masse now.

Fiona Broome says:
24 December 13 at 5:00 am
Dan,

Thanks for your comments.

The turning point in late 2012 is a curious scenario. I will look into that more closely.

I'm always interested in quirky theories. For example, I've read much of "Exo Vaticana," which posits some theories that sounded rather off-the-wall to me, until I saw their supporting evidence. I'm still not sure how seriously to take any of that. The evidence is quirky, but my conclusions might be different. To me, aliens at the Vatican seem a pretty distant reach (no puns intended), but I try to remain objective about all theories. After all, this is kind of a jigsaw puzzle with lots of scrambled pieces, and plenty still missing.

Whatever the answers, something odd is going on, and I'm not sure if this has been the case, all along, or if it's picking up speed now, or what.

Since your experiences include evidence of odd behavior in your sleep, I'm sure you're bright enough to talk with a sleep specialist (or at least your doctor) about it, in case something sleep-related is affecting your waking perceptions, even on a very minor scale. (In all of my paranormal research, I try to rule out normal-ish influences, first. Once that's been addressed and eliminated or reduced as a possibility, I can focus on less mundane explanations.)

I wouldn't leap to the "altered states" conclusion, but take a closer look at how sleep issues could make you more sensitive (aware) of some things in daily life. And, unless sleep is one of your areas of expertise, a specialist might be the best resource for insights.

Your sleep experiences could support theories presented by Dr. Fred Alan Wolf (see my articles tagged with his name: https://mand elaeffect.com/temp/tag/dr-fred-alan-wolf) that when we're dreaming, we may actually be visiting parallel dimensions. If you're visiting not-so-fun ones, or the experience/immersion is especially intense, that could explain the sleep issues and why your reality is differing from others'.

(I'll admit the possibilities seems like a fascinating, real-life Rubik's Cube. And, as a writer, I also see a great fiction series in it... but — as often happens — I'm getting sidetracked.)

The idea of a societal fracture is intriguing. Once again falling back on sci-fi story lines, I'm wondering how video games — and now computer games — might be part of the sorting or conditioning. Then there are the deliberate effects of binaural beats and brain "entrainment," and how those could fit into the mix. (No pun intended.)

I'm intrigued by the possibilities. One thing (among many) that I enjoy about this site are the conversations among bright people who are willing to offer unusual, far-from-the-mainstream theories.

We need more of those. Mundane and mainstream answers aren't working with what we're seeing here.

Thanks for the comments!

Cheerfully,

Fiona

Stormy says:

12 August 15 at 2:23 pm

Okay.... For starters whenever Nelson Mandela died in 2013 I walked into the room (the news was on) and I said, "didn't he already? I thought he died in the 80's?" I clearly remember knowing this as a fact, and remembering him as something of a martyr. I also remember berenstEin bears and Ghadafi... I remember all of these things as FACTS.

Now, into my point with your comment... The past couple of years my family says I have been laughing like a maniac in my sleep or making ungodly noises. The first time my grandmother heard it, she came in to tell me to be quiet and she found me dead asleep and then said I started laughing uncontrollably... Loud enough for them to hear me two rooms over..

I am also well adjusted and mentally stable as far as I know. I'm incredibly confused by all of this...

Cliff says:

18 April 11 at 11:00 pm

I often find myself having conversations with people who do not or differently remember events from the past.

Here are a few,

Big Yella, The corn pops kid.

A trailer for a "Wolverine" Movie int he 80's that was just 3 claw mark slashes making up the W.

The death of Ernest Borgnine

Watching a cartoon as a kid on either Electric Company, Sesame street, School House Rock or Pink Panther that showed what looked like ants walking over an ant hill but as they panned back it was a lil cartoon guy sunbathing on a beach and the ants were walking over a bulge in his pants and a joke about ants in the pants.

Fiona says:
20 April 11 at 9:11 am
Cliff,

Thanks for that list! I'm hoping more people share their alternate memories, as you have, so we can see how widespread specific memories/realities are.

I remember Ernest Borgnine's death awhile ago. At the time, I thought, "Wow... he had to be pretty old. I didn't know he was still around." Borgnine's death didn't surprise me until I later saw him interviewed on TV, and he is (obviously) still alive. (As of April 2011, anyway.)

He's always had such a rubbery, craggy face, I never had a clear impression of his age.

But, when he died, I also remember being surprised that people didn't make a bigger deal about it. I also recall no one mentioning him in the context of his Academy Award-winning performance in the movie, Marty. I thought that was sad, because that performance showed a range of talent far beyond his fame on McHale's Navy.

Your Wolverine reference threw me, because I thought it was just three claw marks, too. However, I'm not a Wolverine enthusiast so, in my case, I might be misremembering.

Thanks again for this list. It's exactly what I'm looking for, to encourage more dialogue about this subject.

Cheerfully,

Fiona

Mick says:

19 April 11 at 1:16 am

I don't know if this qualifies, but I recall vividly that when I was in technical school training in the US Army, in the summer of 1991, I saw the movie Terminator 2 in the theater. What was odd is that I remember seeing a scene in which when they are in an old gas station removing the bullets from the T-101, and John Conner asks if he can learn, the terminator tells him that his CPU read-only memory can be reset to learn new things, so there is a scene in which they do this. In the other versions of this movie I have seen since, this does not occur, and in my research of it, it appears this was a deleted scene which did not make it to the final version! This was 1991, and before DVD movies as far as I remember, or at least they (and their deleted scenes) weren't common. Besides, this was in a theater viewing. I spoke to many people about this scene they never saw, years before it was later shown as part of a DVD deleted scenes! The version I saw can be seen here.

http://www.youtube.com/watch?v=2t_wrtyxFp8

On a side note, I think you should do Coast to Coast Am with this. Very interesting subject and not something I remember anyone ever covering in this manner.

Fiona says:

20 April 11 at 9:01 am

Mick,

Thanks for sharing that extraordinary memory, and for the compliments about my research.

Your memory is unusual, since you were "remembering" a scene that did exist in our world — or it probably did — yet you couldn't have known about it.

That opens the door to several explanations. One is a natural gift for telepathy (or something related) so you knew about the deleted scene because you connected (on a psychic level) with the movie's production team.

The alternative is that you "slid" into a parallel reality where that scene remained in the movie. So, in that realm, you saw a different version of the movie than people in this current reality saw.

Either one is possible, and there are probably other explanations that might work.

I really appreciate that you took the time to share this. And, if/whenCoast to Coast AM asks me to talk on their show, I'll be delighted to share what I've learned about this phenomenon, so far.

I think this is fascinating!

Cheerfully,

Fiona

Marna Ehrech says:

16 May 12 at 9:05 am

Fiona, totally fascinating. IN fact, in my "goddess gathering" to-morrow we are going to be discussing this phenomenon, because I've been watching it for years.

My example:

Many years ago, I was discussing with 2 friends, a couple, while at dinner at their house, his new cell phone number. So I input it in my cell phone, and she told me, "His last name has an unusual spelling," and proceeded to tell me.

So I entered it that way, with an extra vowel, an "i". It is still in my cell phone that way because I never changed it.

A couple years ago, I brought that up in a conversation with them, and they looked at me like I was crazy. "No," he said, "my name does not have an 'i' in it."

I was incredulous!

Fiona says:

16 May 12 at 1:25 pm

Marna,

I agree, this is absolutely fascinating!

What's especially compelling for me is that so many people are very calm and reasonable about this. I'm not seeing a lot of "I'm right and you're wrong," but mostly astonishment.

It's sort of like saying, "The sky is blue." There's no reason to force that opinion on others; we know the sky is basically blue. Some of us know that we saw the news reports of Nelson Mandela's death and funeral; we don't need to prove it to anyone. It's a simple fact for us, and it's kind of a relief to find others with the exact same memories.. whatever that means in terms of shifting realities.

I love it that you have physical evidence like that, in your phone. That adds even more weight to this concept.

Cool stuff, really. I have no idea what any of this means, but... well, it's simply fascinating!

Cheerfully,

Fiona

Cynthia Sue Larson says:

12 July 13 at 7:20 pm

I just discussed this subject on a recent "Coast to Coast" show with George Noory... including the topic of the "alive again" phenomenon, the specific example of Nelson Mandela, and the physics responsible for causing these kinds of reality shifts. I discuss this phenomena in my book, Reality Shifts, and on my RealityShifters website featuring hundreds of these kinds of experiences from people around the world.

Fiona Broome says:

13 July 13 at 4:58 am

Cynthia, good for you! If you're ever speaking at an event where I am, be sure to say hello.

I'm not at Dragon*Con this year due to family priorities, but — if we're in the US — I'll probably be there in 2014. Together, and maybe with a few others who've been studying this, in depth, we might have a fascinating panel.

Jackie says:

28 April 11 at 10:08 am

I remember Nelson Mandela dying in prison. The problem is that I either just knew he did (like it was common knowledge), or it happened at a different time for me. I was born in 1985, so I couldn't have a memory from the early 80s. I think it must have been that it was at a different time, because I remember events after he died... like a really big Oprah episode, concerts in his memory, celebrities ALL wearing his prison numbers, etc.

My experience was that on a regular day, my mom and I were doing separate things with the TV on in the background. I think I was on my laptop and my mom may have also been on hers or reading a book. I believe CNN was the channel the TV was on. Nelson Mandela was mentioned as doing something, which caught both of our ears, I guess, because we both looked up and Nelson Mandela was there... walking around, present day. My mom and I both looked at each other, wide eyed and pale. I was like, "Isn't he dead? I remember him dying...." And she said YES, and we were both discussing how on earth he was alive and no one else was shocked.

We BOTH remembered the Oprah show, we BOTH remembered a specific concert that was live and shown on multiple channels... we both remembered that he died years ago in prison.

We decided it must've been in another dimension or everyone was just as confused as we were, but afraid to sound crazy... or maybe the government brainwashed everyone and just missed us?

I found this site because there's a topic on abovetopsecret.com about time shifts and I wrote about my experience there, then I wondered if anyone else had my same memory (my mom died a few years ago, so now I'm the only one I know with this memory) about him dying and then Googled it. I'm amazed that so many other people have this memory. We couldn't have all slipped into another dimension and remember it. There must be something more logical at work... like he did die, and the forces at work just expected us to not say anything? I have no idea what the explanation is, but I know he died. You could give me a polygraph and I would pass.

Fiona says:

28 April 11 at 11:01 am

Very cool! And, like you, I know I'd pass a polygraph about this.

My leading theory is still that we're regularly sliding into other realms, dimensions or realities. Then, when our memories don't quite fit the world around us, we figure, "Oh, I must have been confused," or misremembered, or something.

However, when it's a big issue — like the death of Nelson Mandela or Billy Graham — it's a lot harder for people to say, "I must have gotten that wrong." As you can see, people remember events like

59

that with so much detail, it's not like they misplaced their car keys or something... this is much, much bigger. They remember what they saw on TV, what friends & family said at the time, and so on.

It's like when President Kennedy died; people in that generation can still tell you exactly where they were and what they were doing when they got the news. They remember the weather, how they reacted, what they did for the rest of the day, and related events that followed it.

These events, like Nelson Mandela's death, had so much impact, people seem to have a massive number of associated memories.

What makes this interesting is when multiple people share the same exact memories. I have a vague memory of the Oprah show, but it wasn't a time when I was watching much TV.

I do remember the big deal about his widow and literary rights, etc. I remember the televised march in South Africa, with people dressed in black and either trying to look brave or sobbing uncontrollably. I remember the banner that was carried at the front of the march, with black, hand-painted lettering on a white background. I remember the widow collapsing, and how very young (and a little frightened) she looked. I remember days of mourning, worldwide. I think that covered three days.

... the quantum explanation works best for me. There are times when I talk with people and it's like the recognition people shared in "Close Encounters...," when they'd all had their own encounters with the aliens. It's like people who've slid into a particular reality have a different energy component around them, or something.

I'm reminded of a church friend in Florida who was in a drawing for a new car. She had to pick the winning key out of a big bowl of keys, and all the keys looked alike. She prayed that the correct key would sort of light up for her, and it did... and she and her husband drove their new car home that afternoon.

They also try to convey that "lighting up" effect visually in the TV show, "Psych."

In real life, I haven't met enough people who remember Nelson Mandela dying, to say that they all have that "lit up" energy. All I know is that many of them have a kind of glow... this is difficult to articulate. There's a recognition, of sorts. I don't remember them, but they share a certain quality.

I get a lot of weird email, so I'm getting pretty good at spotting when someone's simply strange, as opposed to when they're completely normal but telling me a credible (but wild-sounding) story.

What impresses me is how very normal most people are who remember Nelson Mandela dying. Or Billy Graham dying. Or any of a dozen other memories that don't fit our apparent history.

They (like me) know how crazy it sounds to talk about this. They're not necessarily comfortable admitting to any of this.

I remember Nelson Mandela dying in prison. I'm sure your memories are real, too.

What we don't know (yet) is how to explain this. It could be a conspiracy. It could be something quantum. I'm not sure, but as more of us share our stories, I'm hoping we'll see a pattern to this, and find answers.

Thank you so much for sharing your story in such detail!

Cheerfully,

Fiona

Rachel says:

10 November 15 at 8:48 pm

Polygraph tests are not accurate. They are used to track whether or not your heart beat is rising or if you are sweating which, according to the machine, are signs that you are lying. But you could be telling the truth and still be nervous and sweaty with an increased heart rate. Don't trust that a polygraph test can determine whether or not what you are stating is in fact the truth as its inventor deeply regretted inventing it because of the way it was being used by law enforcement.

Fiona Broome says:

11 November 15 at 6:11 am

Rachel, I think you're taking our comments too literally. Well, mine anyway. I don't need a polygraph to inform myself whether or not I'm telling the truth. How polygraphs work is far off-topic, and I only approved this as an example of the kind of comment I'll ordinarily delete. (Rachel, that's why some of your other comments weren't approved.)

Margaret says:

30 May 11 at 7:50 am

In 1967 my high school teacher took our class on a field trip to an experimental farm and showed us a cloned sheep called Dolly. In 1977 I heard on the radio that the first cloned sheep called Dolly had happened. Now it seems that in this timeline it did not happen until 1997. I also remember Nelson Mandela's funeral and the deaths of Billy Graham, Dom Deluis, Ernest Borgenine and Mickey Roomie. It's all very interesting.

Eric says:

12 February 14 at 1:43 am

Not only did the clone Dolly take place in 1977, soon afterward a book about a millionaire (money was worth more then) cloning HIMSELF came out to either capitalize on it or admit to the world that cloning was happening – and it referenced Dolly repeatedly

Colleen says:

13 July 11 at 9:59 pm

I also remember Nelson Mandela dying in prison and was quite amazed when he was elected president of South Africa. Last night I watched the movie, Invictus, and kept wondering where or when was I? I clearly remember the announcement of his death and was amazed that more people around me were not moved by the sadness of it. I also remember vaguely some controversy about his "estate".

There are a few things that do not match my memories of this universe. Such as Honduras. I remember it as an island in the Caribbean, not a country in Central America.

Once, when on the way to church as my husband drove south on the 5 freeway near Los Angeles, I saw what appeared a large crack across the width of the entire freeway – I braced myself for the shock and – nothing. There was no bump or any sensation of the tiniest crack. I had seen it, at least a foot wide. My husband saw nothing, yet just as I began to think I had imagined it I noticed a golf course on the same hill that we had driven past for 10 years. It had not been there before.

Did I experience a crack in time, or a crack between the universes? I am still not sure.

lorrie @ clueless in carolina says:

18 July 11 at 10:27 am

Ernest Borgnine is ALIVE? I KNOW I remember hearing that he died. I follow pop culture very carefully; Hollywood fascinates me.

Nelson Mandela-I remember somebody talking about how his spirit was soaring free from his jail cell. Bill Cosby named his TV grandchildren "Winnie" and "Nelson" and I thought, oh how sweet, he's paying homage to a brave deceased hero.

—— ⚬ ——

ORIGINAL COMMENTS - PART 2

B en Conroy says:
20 July 11 at 6:07 pm

Hi Fiona,

My experience doesnt involve a memory as much as a strange co-incidence. For years I firmly believed there to be 52 states in America. Quite a shock when I found out there was only 50,

After this, I must have asked 25-30 people (in Europe, as I'm Irish), literally everbody I met, how many states in America. Every one said 52. After I said there was 50, their reaction remained 'oh yea. wierd.'

Maybe theres another explanation for it, but occasionally I still ask and hear 52!

I encourage anybody reading this to ask people away from America (who wouldn't know as readily) and see how many times 52 is replied!

Sarah says:
27 November 13 at 7:24 pm

I also remember being asked how many states and was absolutely sure that the answer was 52. When I was told there was only 50 I found it hard to believe. I am also Irish and brushed it off as getting mixed up with 32

louis says:

12 December 13 at 11:25 am

All the above comments come from persons outside the US, but i was born and raised there and I remember getting the answer wrong on tests in school and to this day sometimes get it mixed up because at some point i was sure there were 52 and then at another point just decided to go along with everyone else that its 50.

Also grew up in the 80's and remember the Wolverine ad. I was in my cousin Anthonys house and we were like, wow thats gonna be so awesome, and i remember getting that raw emotional rush of anticipation and excitement of looking forward to a great thing in the future..

Soul says:

10 May 14 at 4:36 pm

Ok, I'm American, and when I was a little kid I was really adamant that there were 52 states and all the adults in my life (since I'm dyslexic) thought that I was just so cute and quirky. And then I saw this Fairly Odd Parents episode where Timmy Turner was asked by the creepy teacher how many states there were and he said "51" and this didn't sound very wrong to me. And then like the in the show it was announced that North and South dekota had made up and joined so there were 51 states and just like.........

This is so a thing that happened. And I thought nothing of it when the thing about Portico joining the US started up because I was older then and instead of being like "There are going to be 53 states maybe ok" I was like "How many states are there?" And I still don't remember 50 as being the number, like I draw a blank instead of thinking it's 52 but like......

I was reading this website for kicks but now I'm really, really creeped out this is so weird. And I remember my dad always asking me how many states there were because I always, always got it wrong and he thought I it was so funny and that I was so stupid.

But I have no idea what the other states would be. If I was asked to list them (I wouldn't be able to) I wouldn't have two extra names.

: Just pulled up the episode, he says "49" and not "52". Here the transcript

http://fairlyoddparents.wikia.com/wiki/Mr._Right!_%28transcript%29

Kurt Robinson says:

13 October 14 at 1:19 am

I'm Australian and I remember it came up as a question at a trivia night. I said 52, because I remembered it from an Ol' Dirty Bastard lyric "To any MC in any 52 states/I get psycho, killer, Norman Bates!" Of course ODB was wrong, and I didn't get the point. I'm not sure if he actually thought there was 52 states or he just said it because it scans better.

thevenerablecorvex says:

12 December 14 at 3:40 am

For what it's worth, there was an episode of Star Trek: The Next Generation where they find an American flag from the mid-twenty-first century with 52 stars (presumably denoting 52 states, including 2 future ones not yet belonging to the union).

I have no idea whether you watch Star Trek or not though,

Angel says:
1 September 11 at 9:53 pm
I remember "tank boy" getting run over by the tank at Tiananmen Square. My husband doesn't. We googled it and apparently he didn't get run over. I have a very vivid memory though. I remember seeing a video of it. I remember learning this in 7th grade history.

Bree says:
28 August 12 at 12:35 pm
I remember TANK BOY getting run over. My partner and myself were talking about Tiananmen Square and tank boy. I mentioned how horrible it was that he was killed, my partner had no memory of that and thought I was crazy. He had to go on YouTube to show me that he lived. As i watched i had no recollection of that event of him living.

James says:
28 September 12 at 11:35 pm
Same here I remember seeing blood on the street after the tank rolled over him and how the backlash nearly caused communism to

fall apart in china and then they switched to the capitalistic command economy. This is so weird.

Scott says:

21 August 14 at 9:42 pm

Guam, the Northern Marianas Islands, and the Us Virgin Islands are US Territories as well. But I agree as a kid I always thought it was 52 states. I had no concept of territories.

Jasper Allen says:

15 October 11 at 3:46 am

I remember Mandelas funeral being on the news in the UK in the late 80's. At the time I was just a kid and I didn't have a clue who Mandela was.

I was also taught at school that America had 52 states.

ggameoverr says:

10 January 12 at 3:32 pm

I too remember Mandela dying in Prison, right before he was to be released. I thought this won't be good, the South Africans will think he was kill or something. It was on CNN Headline news around lunchtime. I was in Highschool so it was in the 80's.

Jonathan says:

31 January 12 at 4:04 am

This is just WEIRD ! The more I think about it, the more REAL the memory becomes. I live in South Africa, was born in 1980 so I would have been a kid. The memory is most certainly there (SOME-THING about his Mandela's death). It's like seriously, "HEY wth" ! Also remember something about Gadaffi dying. Billy Graham for a surety. I test it on my mother and asked her, "you remember Billy Graham dying right ?" To which she replied "Yeah he died from alzymers".(Excuse the speeling there lol). When I informed that he was still in fact alive she said, "oh well then he was in hospital from it".

It's weird, like the men in black movie. I don't believe in parallel universes, but mind altering ? Sure. Go look at some of the documentaries on youtube, in regards to the illuminati, and freemasonary movements or sects. It's actually CRAZY about what they've achieved, assassinated and brain washed in the past to get what they want. (World domination). Thus the new world order. Watch out for your cell phones. Science fiction ? No, science reality.

Next thing we'll see princess diana on tv and know one will remember her death, 911 wouldn't be remembered by most.... Just wack.

Fiona says:

3 March 12 at 5:44 am

Jonathan,

Those are very good points.

My paranormal research is generally based in science, so the quantum concepts of parallel realities work for me.

And, in a spiritual context, I've wondered if the "many mansions" and "many rooms" refer to parallel worlds. The Gospel of John —

the full version, not just what's included in the canonical Bible —
raises many questions about what was going on around the first
century of the current era. Parallel realities, teleportation, and grav-
ity-defying incidents could be what his stories describe. Or, they
could be actual miracles. Generally, I try to avoid bringing theology
into this.

Though I'm not sure what to think about this, I keep going back
to what physics experiments suggest about our world... and the other
worlds that may exist. That's my focus.

However, mind control is also a viable explanation for the Mandela Effect. What doesn't make sense is why Mandela, or Billy Graham, or other incidents... unless it's to make people think they're
quietly losing their minds. The point of that, from a "tin foil hat"
viewpoint...? Well, if you don't trust your own memories and perceptions of reality, you become more dependent on others' collective
explanations of reality. So, the MIB concept is viable. It's also chill-
ing.

I'm more comfortable with the quantum view of this. I still think
these incidents are real, but in other realities.

Nevertheless, your explanation is equally credible, depending on
the individual's beliefs and context for them.

Sincerely,

Fiona

Jade says:

13 November 15 at 2:13 pm

Fiona, do you have a link where I could find the full Gospel of John? You've got me interested, now!

Fiona Broome says:

14 November 15 at 8:40 am

Jade, the best way to find it is to search for "lost gospel of John" and perhaps add "PDF" to your search. In theory, it's so old, the entire manuscript should be in the public domain.

kim wing says:

25 February 12 at 3:43 pm

I also remember reading the newspaper and all the whoopola about Nelson Mandela dying on tv. I remember the banners at his funeral. I am an adult and take such history seriously. When he was released from prison I was flabbergasted. Art bell also bought this up on one of his shows and if he hadn't I still would have been thinking I was goofy. this happened folks. The Freddy Prince baby with Sarah also was in the news. I was so happy for him, since I loved his dad. But hay this didn't happen either huh? What the heck, being a strong christian I will leave this to Jesus!

Ron says:

26 February 12 at 1:32 am

I remember Nelson Mandella dying while in prison, and I also re-member that his wife became president there sometime afterwards. Later on I heard a radio show with someone talking about this subject, that others too remember his death.

Inquiring Mind says:

2 March 12 at 10:23 pm

I remember it too.

I was only a kid — I was born in 1983 — but I remember seeing something about his death on TV once when I was waiting for Saturday morning cartoons to come on. It was like a biography/memorial/documentary thing. I had no idea who he was, but for some reason it made an impression on me. What I specifically remember is that A) he was in prison at some point, and B) that he passed away.

Years later, as a teenager, I remember having a few moments of "Wait, what? I thought he died!" ...But it wasn't until recently that I discovered I'm not alone in my recollection!

Mary says:

3 March 12 at 12:19 am

I have a memory of a scene in the movie Queen of the Damned that isn't in the movie or deleted scenes sections or whatever its called on the disk.. I can't quite remember how it goes but I remember watching it at my cousin's house for the first time and remembering this.. difference/extra scene , or something. But she doesn't remember even watching the movie.

Fiona says:

3 March 12 at 5:09 am

Mary,

Your comment fascinated me, because I saw Queen of the Damned when it had more in it. In fact, a friend and I sat through it twice, because the use of color in the movie was so clever: With each transition in the plot, it was like more colors were added to the palette. For example, I think the first club scene was where bottle green hue was added, and it remained in the movie for most of the scenes that followed.

Then, we went out for coffee and talked about it, at length. As an artist, colors inspire me, and the use of color in this movie fascinated me. (I can remember how impressed I was with the use of the color red to highlight intense scenes in the original movie, Dr. Zhivago. Otherwise, it was predominantly b&w and shades of gray.)

So, I know exactly what I saw.

However, when I saw Queen of the Damned on cable TV — I don't recall which of the premium channels had it — the movie was really different. I'd assumed the theatrical release (which had done badly) had been modified in an attempt to sell more DVDs or something.

Now, I'm wondering if it was a "Mandela moment" as my husband and I call it. In my case, it may still be a case of the DVD being ed from the theatrical release, but the underlying concept remains: I think some/many/all of us are "sliding" more often than we may realize.

Sincerely,

Fiona

Natasha Davis says:

7 December 13 at 2:23 pm

I'm finding this thread very intresting ...we moved into the house were in a few years ago and I dreamt about this house well before we even knew about also before I was what I'm calling awake ...

Gurluas says:

12 February 14 at 1:37 pm

Assuming that OBE's are real, then it's possible that our consciouness may touch with other versions of ourselves, and since time isn't linear, you may very well touched the consciousness of another you, who in that reality's present, lived in that house.

Michelle S says:

3 March 12 at 3:50 am

i remember in 2nd grade (im currently 32) making african flags at school and putting them in the hallway and my teacher was from s africa so she took it really hard and we had a fund drive at school to fly her home, we made t shirts with his prison number on it and wore them when she arrived back. gosh am i crazy. this is freaky, i have an excellent memory i am not crazy, or am i...please delete this site it has me questioning my sanity, so hes not dead?!!!! i dont remember him being released from prison, i just googled around and he was released. ogosh i feel like im going nuts!!!!!

Fiona says:

3 March 12 at 5:17 am

Michelle,

You're not crazy. People with these memories... we have very specific, complete, and detailed memories. It's not a case of, "Gee, I must have forgotten that." We have too many associated, distinct, and clear memories associated with Mandela's death, or whatever it is that we remember.

This site is staying up [for now]. This is too important not to talk about.

The alarm you're feeling is also consistent when people make this discovery. They have memories — very clear, real memories — that don't fit the timeline they're in.

They live normal lives. Most of their memories match other people's. They can chat with a family member and talk about an event they shared in the past, and all the memories match. And, they can do this over & over again.

Then, there's something like the Mandela memory... and it's completely out-of-character in the context of their other memories. It's the one that doesn't fit, and it doesn't fit at all. It's an anomaly that people can't work with, except to feel like they're losing their minds.

So, this site is here because the phenomenon is too distinct to brush off as "a mental lapse" or anything like that.

Sincerely,

Fiona

CJ Pronti says:

3 March 12 at 4:12 am

Hi! I know that this is an old article, but I have something to add that may be related. I remember for many years, from childhood until just recently, that New Zealand was below and to the East of Australia, instead of Northeast as it is now. I was shocked to recently see that it was in a new position. In school, I excelled in Geography, and I used to study atlases as a hobby. I know in my heart that it used to be below Australia. Since finding out the location as it is now, I have found some others who remember New Zealand being located Southeast of Australia. I hope that you find this useful! It is very strange.

Fiona says:
3 March 12 at 5:21 am
CJ,
Wow... thanks for posting that! I hadn't heard of any geographical memories, so this fascinates me.

Like most people, I've heard others look at a map and exclaim, "Wow! I always thought [some country] was in a different place!" And, until now, I'd always figured their geography skills were weak.

However, speaking in quantum terms (string theory, m theory, etc.), geography could be different in other, parallel realities.

That never crossed my mind. Very cool, and I'm going to adjust my judgment of others when I hear one of those comments in the future. Maybe their geography skills are fine, and it's simply the "Mandela Effect" they're experiencing.

Thanks for posting this!
Cheerfully,
Fiona

Scott says:

13 May 12 at 10:08 am

I'm also a big geography guy and New Zealand is STILL east and mostly south of Australia, definitely not northeast! Just double checked on google maps and its where I always remembered it. Was your post entered in a different reality from mine, or can you please double check and correct yourself?

Fiona says:

13 May 12 at 11:38 am

Scott,

You're a big geography guy, and so it probably seemed unsettling to see someone talking about New Zealand in another location. In your time stream/s, New Zealand hasn't moved.

For others, maybe it has. There's nothing to "correct." We can't fix those other time streams (or the one we're in). For now, we respect the intelligence of those whose memories are from those other realities.

Around 1990, I can recall looking at a map to find the homeland of a Maori friend. New Zealand was northeast of Australia, slightly larger than and not far from Papua New Guinea.

Today, I checked it on Google Maps, and — as you said — it's southeast of Australia. It's also considerably smaller than I recall, and a different shape. (It was also different from Papua New Guinea, so it's not that I mixed up two "New _____" names.)

Finding conflicting data in this time stream doesn't negate the past reality. There's nothing to correct.

Sure, it could be a mistake or a faulty memory, but that's an argument many of us have already presented to ourselves. It didn't really work. Not long-term, anyway.

Mistakes and faulty memories are usually simple to accept. At the time, we weren't paying close attention. Or, we took our data from someone else without verifying their information.

They're usually different in quality when contrasted with alternate memories. If we knew how to double-check those alternate facts (or maps) in that time stream, we would.

Meanwhile, there's comfort in finding others who share our vivid, dimensional memories from other realities.

Cheerfully,

Fiona

Scott says:

15 May 12 at 8:05 am

Hi Fiona and thanks for adding this additional insight. I had no idea you also remembered New Zealand somewhere else and totally respect that someone else may have experienced this on another timeline. I find all this fascinating especially considering that I definitely recall Jack Palance dieing far sooner than he actually did and found others who experienced that on other blogs (see my posting on this below).

I also want to point out that the original poster on this New Zealand topic, above, actually said this:

"New Zealand was below and to the East of Australia, instead of Northeast as it is now"

This is interesting since it is the inverse and mine (and apparently yours) current reality. Did this poster make a mistake, and actually mean to say New Zealand is NOW southeast of Australia, or did they somehow post to this SAME site from a whole other timeline?

Fiona says:

16 May 12 at 1:20 pm

Hi,

The Jack Palance death is one I've heard regularly from people I discuss this with, offline. I've had to use a phone (or other, nearby Internet connection) to show Jack Palance's actual obit to them, just as I often have to show that Billy Graham's funeral did not, in fact, occur when some people think it did.

It is possible that people are posting here from another timeline. (Whether or not that's likely is another topic.) It'd be more than a little weird, but a digital crossover from another timeline... that seems more plausible to me than the actual physical differences (dates and events, offline) that they're reporting.

The more reports I hear, at this website and offline, the more I'm accepting the "Sliders" concept. For someone like me, who generally looks for confirmation and something resembling hard evidence, that's a major leap.

In my opinion, the reports here barely scratch the surface. I'd have figured my NZ geography memories were false, except that others raised the question here. In fact, I'd never have started this website at all, if someone (in the "green room" at Dragon*Con) hadn't brought up the Nelson Mandela memories as something others experienced. I was perfectly happy thinking I'd managed to absolutely misinterpret something else, and dub-in (fairly extensively) Mandela's identity.

There's a potential for many other "false" memories that occurred in other timelines, but not in the one described by Wikipedia and the news reports in this timeline.

For me, one of the most interesting things is that — unlike the TV series, "Sliders" — I'm not seeing reports of cues that the timeline shifted. People don't say things like, "When I saw the Billy Graham funeral, other things seemed kind of odd at the time." The later responses are fairly consistently, "Whoa. Did I misremember that... or what...?" They're baffled.

The alternate memories — and/or reality shift/s since then — don't seem to be accompanied by anything dramatically different in context. What's weird for people is when they find out that the memory doesn't fit this reality. It's not that the memory itself had any significantly weird moments in it; the Roman legions didn't conquer the world and remain in power, Hitler didn't succeed, and so on. In other words, the things we see on SyFy (etc.) shows that indicate a different timeline... the cues aren't there.

And, for most of us, our initial reaction is to try to frame it into a memory lapse or a misunderstanding, rather than accept that our memories are accurate but from another timeline.

When I have just a little more time for this, I want to survey to see how many people remember multiple events from alternate time streams, or if most people have just one of these jarring memories.

It's fascinating!

Cheerfully,

Fiona

Gut says:

12 September 12 at 8:50 am

I have a clear and distinct memory of NZ being north east of australia not south east. I can remember a map of the world in a classroom from a few years ago. I have the memory because I always thought I'd like to go there someday because being a UK centric map, it seemed so far away and it would have been really cool to go there. I don't know, maybe my memory is slightly corrupted, but as I read your exchanges it shocked me slightly to read.

Maria says:

11 October 15 at 8:04 pm

Absolutely I remember New Zealand being NE of Australia. In 1981 I was selected to be a foreign exchange student. My second choice was New Zealand so I did a lot of research on the country at the library. That's strange for a whole country to move, and to be a slightly different shape.

Joe says:

3 March 12 at 1:13 pm

I have read about that vanishing Star Trek episode before years ago on some discussion forum, but can't remember the details. Do you have a description by chance? I swear I remember looking it up and remembering it being aired but not being able to find a description anywhere, much like the person mentioned above.

I'll add a couple, and this is one I remember VERY clearly: Sometime in the 90's, I heard that Robert Crumb had died, and I discussed it with a big RC fan who was very sad about it. Some years later, he was (and is still) very much alive.

One more thing, when John Lennon was shot, I remember it being on Dec. 10, 1980. Watching TV all day the next day, I saw that death date on the bottom of the screen, it was burned into my memory. Now, and for the past few years from my perspective, he died on Dec. 8 1980.

Thanks for the great site!

Fiona says:

3 March 12 at 1:59 pm

Joe,

Thanks for describing the things you remember. I think the more we share those memories and connect with others who also recall them, the better we'll feel about all of this... even if it's more than a little weird.

I can tell you more about the Star Trek episode, as I overheard the conversation:

The fan was talking with Robert Beltran, and the fan said how happy he and his wife had been, when the Chakotay character was "brought back" into the story. The fan said how disappointed they'd been, when the character had been killed off.

That fan — with his wife by his side — asked Robert Beltran why there hadn't been an explanation in the story. They said that

Chakotay had just reappeared, as if he'd never died and never been out of the Star Trek series at all.

Mr. Beltran looked at the fan, confused, and said that Chakotay hadn't been killed during the series, and so there was no "return" to explain.

Both the fan and his wife did their best to take this in stride, but I could see that they were baffled. That's why I decided to talk with them, give them my card, and tell them that — if they had other questions — to let me know.

This was a moment when it wasn't just one person's memory. It was the memory of two people, who were in complete agreement about what they'd seen on the TV.

As I left them, they were still trying to figure out what it was that they actually saw, because neither of them had another explanation for something they remembered so clearly.

When these things happen, the logical assumption is, "Oh, I must have been mistaken." However, when there are two people in complete agreement, and they both experienced the event, this becomes unsettling.

I hope that's helpful.

Sincerely,

Fiona

Ironic says:
6 May 13 at 2:34 pm
Actually, in the final episode 'Endgame', Chakotay did die, but it was an alternate reality, if you can believe that. His wife Seven of

9 was killed and when he returned to Earth it is implied he killed himself. Janeway goes back in time and changes it so Seven and he live. How's that for ironic??

Fiona Broome says:

6 May 13 at 3:16 pm

Wow, that is ironic! I hadn't watched the every season of the show when I spoke with Mr. Beltran, so I didn't know about "Endgame."

However, the couple who "remembered" him dying, remembered it as a mid-series episode, and they remembered him returning with no explanation, several episodes later.

So, they weren't mis-remembering the last episode. In fact, the couple having the conversation were the kinds of people who remember every episode, every character, and probably know the writers of their favorite episodes. They were very normal people, just enthusiastic ST:V enthusiasts.

(I'm pretty good at recognizing the kinds of people you edge away from, tactfully, and let them ramble and rave about certain things. This particular couple... they were nearly the polar opposite of that. They looked like the kinds of parents you'd see at a PTA meeting, and they'd blend right in.)

Jordanes says:

3 March 12 at 10:42 pm

Here's one...

A lot of people clearly recall a picture of Henry VIII holding a turkey leg. Think about it and you'll remember seeing it.

The problem is...no such picture exists. Search for it; you won't find it.

Sez says:

28 June 12 at 4:18 pm

There is a Simpson's episode that parodies this. I wonder if it was inspired by this train of thought, or if it is what originated it.

Fiona Broome says:

28 June 12 at 4:25 pm

Sez, how funny! I've never watched The Simpsons, but this discussion has been active — offline, before I launched this website — for over five years. And, we were discussing it in the "green room" at Dragon*Con, among quite a few writers and producers. So, someone might have glommed onto it there. (However, I don't think the Henry VIII/turkey leg memory was part of those discussions.)

It's just as likely that they heard about this elsewhere. My website doesn't have a monopoly on the topic. As the comments suggest, a whole lot of people have these alternate memories.

Amanda says:

16 December 13 at 6:11 pm

I know I'm rather late to the party, but in case you get e-mail notifications or something: There's a picture of Henry VIII holding a turkey leg on the cover of Horrible Histories: Terrifying Tudors. Depending whether this is the picture you remember, this is either an explanation of your memory or a possible indication that the person who drew it might share that memory with you.

Fiona Broome says:

17 December 13 at 5:37 am

Amanda, thank you! I do own a copy of that book, and — in my case — it might explain my memory. It depends on how closely it resembles the Holbein-style works, and the details (colors of his clothing, which hand holds the turkey leg, etc.). Coincidentally, I'm reorganizing my stored books this week, so I'm likely to see the book.

I'm always looking for reasonable explanations I hadn't considered. In most cases, there are no reasonable explanations. However, depending on how the book cover strikes me when I see it, this may explain the Henry Tudor + turkey leg memory.

It may not explain Americans' memories of that painting. I'm fairly certain the Horrible Histories books aren't widely available in the U.S. (I bought my copies in England.)

Still, it's something to consider.

Thanks again!

Cheerfully,

Fiona

Amanda says:

17 December 13 at 9:47 am

Sorry for the first version of this comment (and my original comment) being in the wrong place – I'm used to other sites where the Reply button's at the end of a comment!

Having read more of the site, and your comment, I don't think it even explains your memory. (It may well explain mine, though – I'm pretty good at getting muddled and mixing things up!) The Horrible Histories cover is a cartoon; you can see it on the Amazon page (http://www.amazon.co.uk/Terrifying-Tudors-Horrible-Histories-Terry/dp/1407104225/). I also hadn't realised they were a UK-specific thing. I guess this counts as potential evidence, then, rather than an explanation!

Thanks for making this site! It's fascinating reading ?? I definitely thought there were 52 states for a long time (and even having discovered otherwise a few years ago, if you asked me how many there were I'd still probably say 52 most of the time). My dad was surprised when I told him last night – he thought there were 51.

Whilst I was born in 1990 and never paid much attention to the news as a kid anyway, so I don't remember any particular coverage of Mandela's death before, I did think he'd died ages ago.

Fiona Broome says:
18 December 13 at 7:08 am
Hi, Amanda!
Thanks so much for linking to the Horrible Histories book. That saves me the effort of finding my copy.

Looking at it.. you're right. It doesn't explain my memory. Mine is a Holbein-style painting, full face, looking straight at the artist, holding the turkey leg. The clothing looks close to correct on the book cover, so — again — I think you may be right about the "missing" painting inspiring that cover. I'll see if I can contact the cover artist to see what he or she recalls.

The number of states fascinates me. I can almost date how old someone is, by how many states they first say when asked the number. Someone born in the 1950s or 1960s will say 50 or 51. Someone born later will usually say 52, if not 50. In-between, people will often say 51 states, and then correct themselves to 52, and the usual 52nd (that they'd forgotten) is Puerto Rico.

While my memories are firm about 50 states (and only 50), the volume of people who say 51 or 52 — and how well their answers relate to their ages — is interesting.

At this point, it's too small a sampling and entirely anecdotal, but still... it's fascinating!

Thanks again!

Cheerfully,

Fiona

Joe says:

3 March 12 at 11:31 pm

Fiona,

Thanks very much for the description of your friends' Start Trek Voyager memory. I used to never miss that show, but at the same time it has been a few years, and so I don't remember it with enough sharpness to say either way that there was a Chakotay death or not.. Although length of time is not necessarily a factor either, as the episode I was thinking of was from the old first version with Captain

Kirk et al. I watched those so many times as a kid, so if anything was out of place, it would stick out.

Don, if we slip into a different timeline, then for the *most* part it would seem that our memories are of the new timeline, we would always remember the new reality with its history as "real". Remembering a piece of an old reality is perhaps not how it's supposed to work, or alternately, the way it should work, who knows. If this is true, that we jump realities, then there will be no proof in the sense there will be newspaper articles of Nelson Mandela dying that can be dug up somewhere, all the artifacts from the old reality do not exist here..

Another one, I remember "Mystery Science Theater 3000" being instead "MST 2000". I honestly thought they had changed the name for some reason, like 3000 sounded more futuristic or something, but no.. Always been 3K.

Nothing Is Real – John Lennon. ??

Trunk says:

4 March 12 at 2:57 am

Just briefly, I remember the movie se7en, with Brad Pitt and Morgan Freeman?

I distinctly remember the villain being played (very well I night add) by John Malcovich!

I remember hundreds of frames of his face, the end scene (head reveal) is burnt into my memory.

Thing is, around 12 years later I notice Kevin Spacey played this part! And badly! WTF?

So clear in my memory, that I actually started researching whether there had been some form of lawsuit between Malcovich and the publishing company, and if demanded to be removed from the film.. Thus spacey resulting in a reshoot of Johns original role... Alas, this was not the case,

People just never remembered Malcovich in the role..

If one person shares this memory with me, please speak up.

colette says:

24 January 13 at 9:25 pm

hi ,i have watched the film a few times ,the last time being about 2 years ago.and yes john malcovich was the in the movie as the killer. i was so shocked when you said he wasnt in the film that i have just googled it and you are right , but i know he was in the film i even remember his voice as he was really creepy . im actually lost for words. i also remember early last year of watching the obituaries for kirk douglas on the news,and mickey rooney about 14 years ago .

Ann says:

27 June 13 at 8:47 am

I loved the movie seven. I have an old VHS copy and it was definitely John Malcovich who played the role of the killer! I remember this because I am a huge fan of his. I have lots of random memories of things other people don't remember.

Rob says:

4 March 12 at 3:31 am

I distinctly remember Luke Skywalker missing with his grapple line on the first try when they were escaping across the Death Star chasm when I saw the original Star Wars in the theater in 1977 and Leia tersely told him, "Fine hero you are." I remember the audience "awww" when he missed and "yay" when he made it on the second attempt. There are quite a few comments here I remember also.

xt says:

4 March 12 at 4:56 am

Maybe there are infinite parallel universe, you could change to another dimension just by yours desicions!... Just imaging the implications of knowing this...

Lin says:

4 March 12 at 10:45 am

I was shocked to read what CJ Pronti has said.

I experienced the same thing, except the other way around.

I remembered that New Zealand was located North East of Australian East coast, and then now recognised it exists in South East.

I had just a check by googling "world map 2012", sure enough there are many images of NZ locating Sth Est of Aus.

I decided I must have wrongly memorised about the location of NZ (so it would be within this 30 years if slipping happened for me) as I first studied as I was a kid, when I realised I was "wrong" later.

I remembered about it as I have this memory of explaining the location of NZ to a family friend, when I visited him with my family to distant place.

But hearing CJ's comment, it kind of reminded me of the "weird" sensation I felt when I discovered my "mistake" later.

As I come across the current maps numerous times since I thought I made mistake, I had learned to take it in as THE CORRECT INFORMATION and never doubted about it since.

————————

CJ Pronti says:

3 March 12 at 4:12 am

Hi! I know that this is an old article, but I have something to add that may be related. I remember for many years, from childhood until just recently, that New Zealand was below and to the East of Australia, instead of Northeast as it is now. I was shocked to recently see that it was in a new position. In school, I excelled in Geography, and I used to study atlases as a hobby. I know in my heart that it used to be below Australia. Since finding out the location as it is now, I have found some others who remember New Zealand being located Southeast of Australia. I hope that you find this useful! It is very strange.

Jeff says:

4 March 12 at 4:06 pm

So Billy Graham didn't die? I distinctly remember hearing about his death! I really can't be sure about Mandella though I did he was dead, I remember hearing about Ernest Borgnine dying, but he is still alive apparently!

Original Comments - Part 3

B lob says:
      4 March 12 at 4:07 pm

New Zealand has not moved, it is still south and east of Australia, it will not move because it is glued down.

Honduras was called British Honduras I think, and upon gaining independance was re named Belize ?

Billy Graham is dead,yes? if not, please provide a link, i remember him passing about a year or two ago, as does my wife.

Robert Stack passed away, has there been a Robert Stack sighting or something ?

Earnest Borgnine has left us, he was a great actor !

Or am I wrong ? Statements are one thing but evidence to the contrary is another, Links ?

This is a very interesting subject and your Web site is neat, it is a subject that keeps coming back, we often have those "No way ! he died years ago !" moments.

As I am oldish,50, I do remember that Mandella was in prison and he got out and became president of South Africa in the first post aparteit elections, I believe he also passed away in the last 24 months or so, am I wrong? (Aparteit,spell check).

Are you suggesting that Mandella is still alive or that he died again
?

Jimmy Swaggart, the Tellyvangelist, he died, No?

Jerry Lee Lewis was his cousin, they grew up together, (Wow, I'm old !) Jerry Lee was one of the first rockstars.

Chuck Berry is still alive ? As is Keith Richards of the Stones, these guys lived hard lives and were culturally influential, yet I have had friends and aquaintances pass away before they were 30 or 40, life is strange.

Jim Fixx was a Jogging and health Guru in the 1970's and early 80's, he sold books on health, nutrition, Jogging etc;

He was out jogging one day and dropped dead from a heart attack, I think he was about 42 years old.

So one guy eats ultra healthy, does it all right and drops dead,

another guy has his blood changed in Tijuana (true story), so he can kick his Heroin addiction, who lives, who dies ?

God decides .

Sorry if I have gone off topic but you have got my little Sunday afternoon, 3 beer brain, thinking.

Let me tell you about my reverse Elvis moment

Fiona says:

5 March 12 at 6:00 am

Hi, Blob,

The fastest way to check if a celebrity is dead or alive is to go to Wikipedia. The contributors to that site are usually pretty fast to update the vital statistics on celebrities.

As of this morning, Billy Graham is elderly but still in this timestream: http://en.wikipedia.org/wiki/Billy_Graham

Ditto, Ernest Borgnine: http://en.wikipedia.org/wiki/Ernest_B orgnine

Robert Stack left in 2003, but I've heard others who "remembered" his death, years earlier.

The frequency of these specific reports makes me wonder if there is a particular timestream or reality that we slip into more readily than others, and — in that one — all of those people died much earlier than in this reality.

Or, maybe we're sliding through multiple realities regularly, and our current one — where Graham and Borgnine are still alive — is one of the few realities in which those men didn't die earlier.

There are so many possibilities, perhaps one for each reality that physics suggests may exist.

I liked the earlier comment by Joe, about how this may work. Maybe some people don't hit the memory "reset" button when they slide, as well as others do. (Or maybe it's a conscious choice, from an external point from which we're watching ourselves have this (apparently) physical experience.

The realities in which Billy Graham (and others) died..? It might be one we've visited while sleeping, and that reality's (or realities') history was retained as a factual memory, without the memory of the "dream." (After all, most people don't seem to recall most of their dreams.) This would fit with Dr. Fred Alan Wolf's speculations about what dreams are. (See his book, The Dreaming Universe, this excerpt from an interview especially starting at 6:36, or

his Q&A, http://www.fredalanwolf.com/myarticles/The%20Drea
ming%20Universe%20Q&A.pdf, or — for science geeks like me, an
early, simple thesis, http://www.fredalanwolf.com/myarticles/drea
ming%20universe%20paper.pdf.)

Of course, that also takes us into deep quantum and philosophical
territories, questioning the nature of matter and reality, and if this
is all a holodeck. And, if that's the case, it's reasonable to consider
whether dreams take us to other holodecks for contrasting experiences. (If we are, indeed, spiritual beings having a human experience,
I see no theological conflicts with this.)

For me, this is fascinating. I feel that these rich, vivid, uncharacter-
istic memories are evidence of something we don't fully understand
yet. I'm just not sure what.

Cheerfully,

Fiona

Brian says:

15 September 15 at 8:26 am

"...Maybe some people don't hit the memory "reset" button when
they slide, as well as others do. (Or maybe it's a conscious choice,
from an external point from which we're watching ourselves have
this (apparently) physical experience."

Or, it gets jammed. Mine has been jammed, but good by some
traumatic events around the same time.

Teri says:

5 March 12 at 8:09 pm

I saw this subjected posted on another site with a link to this site. My mom and I both also "remember" Mandela dying in prison as well as Billy Graham dying soon after retiring. I can't think of any other specific celebrities but I know there have been times when a celebrity has been brought up on TV or in a magazine or something and I have thought, "Wait...didn't he/she die YEARS ago?"

I haven't read all the comments but a thought that came to me is: It is theorized/suggested that the shadow governments have all this ET technology which includes time machines. Could it be possible that the reason some people remember certain events happening and others don't, and/or there is no documented evidence of these events happening, is because someone "traveled through time" and changed events that happened...but some of us still have the residual memories of these previous events?

I don't know for sure what "Sliders" are but if I get the gist of what I have read it means momentarily slipping out of our reality into another one? If so I have had several situations like that. The ones I can remember are, 1) when I was 12 or 13 I was in an explosion. At the time of the explosion I was standing about 2 feet away from the campfire and my mom was sitting right in front of me. When the explosion happened I somehow disappeared and then reappeared about 25 feet away. I was found near the 5th wheel camper that my parents friends were staying in and nobody can figure out how I got from where I had been standing to where my dad found me. I was conscious, I couldn't breathe because of the smoke and ash in the air from the explosion, and when I was finally able to inhale enough to scream I was far away from where I should have been. It was suggested that I walked/stumbled to the camper but there were numerous obstacles I would have had to get through to get there and my eyes were badly burned from the explosion and I couldn't see anything, so like I said, nobody can figure out how I got to where I was found. 2) That following winter my dad took us Disneyland for Christmas vacation. I was sick with pneumonia the entire time were gone so I don't really have any memories of the trip. I do, however, have one very vivid memory of the trip home. We were in a motorhome and I was sitting on the couch looking out the window at all the snow. There was a turn-off plowed out on the side of the road. I saw the turn out and at the very back, where the snow was piled up, I distinctly saw a decapitated horses head with blood all around it and the snow was covered in blood. I let out a scream and scared the hell out of my parents. I was babbling about this horse head (my mom remembers this happening) but they didn't see anything. 3) I was driving through a town that I traveled through weekly when going to visit my son. One time I was suddenly struck with the sensation that I wasn't where I was supposed to be. Everything was where it was supposed to be but it just looked and felt "different" and I wondered if I had taken a wrong turn and was on the wrong street. This sensation continued until I got to the far end of town then it felt right again. And 4) there was a situation where my mom and I were sitting at an intersection waiting for the oncoming traffic to pass so she could turn. There was a white car behind a semi then the road was clear to turn. The semi passed but there was no white car. I said, "where did the white car go?" My mom said, "You saw it, too?" BOTH of us saw this white car. There were no roads or driveways where this car could have turned, but the damned thing just disappeared! That one still makes my mom and I wonder.

Jodi says:

12 March 12 at 12:03 am

I remember Mandalas death and watching the news about it and showing his cell at the time we only had two tv channels in New Zealand if you want to see if you could find the footage?

Siphakeme says:

28 March 12 at 12:40 am

The mistery of the South African political prisoner who died (was killed) in the 1980's is Steven Bantu Biko! He didn't actually die in prison he was killed by the police while in his holding cell- he had been charged with treason (as all anti-Apartheid activists were in that era).

There was a huge funeral procession and big white banners and a grieving wife, yes, all correct as per the majority 'memory' here. I wad born in the early 80s too and we did nt have a tv so I the only way I have come top know of this is through History and story telling. My family has been quite active in the fight for political freedom in our country so I would say my sources are correct.

I would like to just say that I do not dispute what most of you may/not have 'seen/ experienced' as we live in a complex universe and Biblically we believe and understand that 'all things are possible (through Christ)' and the power of the mind is not fully understood.

*i grew studying that the US has 52 states too

*and New Zealand seems to have 'shifted' in fact my brother and I commented on that in the last Rugby World Cup (last year)! Interesting times we live in, indeed ??

Fiona says:

28 March 12 at 7:39 am

Siphakeme,

Thanks for the comment. I recall Steven Bantu Biko's murder. That's not what I'm remembering as I recall Nelson Mandela's death in prison.

However, I appreciate the reference, in case some readers look at that and say, "Oh. Wait. That might the person and events I'm confusing with Mandela."

For me, there's no question: I remember the news coverage of Nelson Mandela's death. It was definitely Mandela, not someone else.

Sincerely,

Fiona

c says:

29 April 12 at 2:38 am

i vividly remember man on a ledge (it's coming out soon, i think) coming out a really long time ago. and when the movie titan a.e. was released in theatres, i remember seeing previews for it years before.

i was just a kid then so i didn't pay much attention to news but i do have some weird memories about movies. and i do believe i heard about billy graham's death. i'm sorry i have nothing more to contribute but this article is really freaking me out right now. it makes me wonder how much control i really have over my own memories. sometimes i feel like i let too many errant thoughts slide, and don't think consciously enough for myself. you never know what gets through the cracks when you are not paying attention . . .

Lena says:

4 October 13 at 7:26 pm

I remember the same thing with the movie Speed. Granted, I was in elementary school at the time but I recall my parents mentioning something about wanting to rent the movie. Isn't that the movie about the bus that won't stop? Yes, they said.

I know mom and dad only really liked renting new releases, so I asked why they were renting an old movie. They said it was brand new and it had just come out. They chalked up my "memory" of the movie to the fact that I might have seen a trailer in TV. I swear, though — I knew it'd been out for years and it really felt like I'd seen it before.

Also in elementary school, my dad took me to the movie theater to see Monkey Trouble. I'd been dying to see it — I loved animals, especially ones that interacted with humans meaningfully. Anyway, after the movie started, I realized that I'd seen it already. I told my dad, and he said there's no possible way I could have seen it before.

It was new in theaters. I knew the plot and I knew what was going to happen in each scene. I knew much of the dialogue, too.

Fab says:

4 May 12 at 12:26 am

I was very young at the time but am 100% certain that Mandela passed while in prison. I recall all the press dedicated to his life and memory so vividly that when news that he was being released came over the air waves I was stunned and immediately went searching for answers only to find out I wasnt alone. I agree that there must be time line ripple effects that some of us are not aware occur. I've had gaps of missing time and dreams so real I can still recall how things felt when I touched them! Glad i'm not alone!

Kassia says:

15 May 12 at 4:04 pm

Interesting on so many levels. I am in the same boat in regards to Mandela, Billy Graham, Australia!, 52 States (I am European),etc, etc. Here is another thing. I do not remember that there were two atomic bombs, I only know about Hiroshima. All for a sudden people talk about it, like there were always two (Hiroshima and Nagasaki). I could go on and on about the things which are off since of late, but there is one thing nobody ever talks about:

All those people who remember things different than how they are in this moment, this world, have they had a near death experience? This to me is the most important question! What if in this world we survived, but in another we died? Since I had my near death experience, things are not the same anymore. Near death btw in a way, where by law I should have died. How about others?

phoenix says:

21 August 12 at 7:42 pm

you know, i've heard a couple other stories like yours on other boards, and this is absolutely something that i've been wondering about. i am so intrigued by this stuff! i don't have any personal stories about this phenomenan, but its so interesting to me. i know there have been times where i absolutely swear i knew something, and was proven wrong, but i dont even remember the situations, because i just assumed i was wrong, and converted. i have had a couple crazy situations in my life including one car accident... i don't know, though... i remember a ton of details from my childhood that still line up perfectly. sometimes its hard to tell if people change around you, or if you just finally see them for what they are.

phoenix says:

21 August 12 at 7:43 pm

but yes, absolutely, the near death experience thing bears closer attention. 100%. might be the key to this whole thing.

Diana says:

11 February 14 at 3:09 am

Wow. I did have a near-death experience right around the same time I started feeling like I was in the wrong place somehow. I was pushed down a flight of concrete stairs, and I remember thinking I would die. And I landed flat on my back on concrete, with my legs jammed up against a fence. But somehow I got right up. And now the world is different in some minor details. This is amazing to think about!

Rick says:

29 November 15 at 10:08 pm

I have had an NDE also It was Sept 15 2001. I too wonder if that has anything to do with it.

Joe says:

12 June 12 at 10:10 pm

I just last month had a discussion with a friend. I swore Billy Graham died and I watched his funeral on TV and so many people in tears and the sadness of such a great man being laid to rest and being honored by the Presidents and I even remember Bill Clinton speaking words in his honor...my friend said I was crazy. I asked my mother and she remembers us talking about his passing. I just don't know what to think...

Elaine says:

12 June 12 at 10:49 pm

This is all fascinating! I distinctly remember Ernest Borgnine dying and was just jolted to read in these comments that he is alive – I went to Wikipedia immediately to confirm. I grew up watching McHale's Navy, and I had a little girl's crush on him and have loved him as an actor ever since. I also thought Billy Graham was gone, for sure, seeming to recall something with his son speaking, etc.

I love quantum physics, and I have been reading quite a bit in this area for some years now, so the alternate realities/parallel universes idea appeals to me. I also have had other memories that are distinctly different from family members in my personal life (and I am known for an above average memory) that I have suspected are due to reality shifts. Thanks for bringing this all out!

Skye says:

13 June 12 at 10:42 pm

Running across this string via FaceBook seems so odd to me, but here I am...

I remember Billy Graham dying & I was also jolted by the comment about Honduras. I have always thought it was an island also.

I completely believe in multiple timelines; in fact I have had clear recollections of meeting myself at ages 16 & 8. (The 16 y/o me went to the timeline of the 8 y/o me. The teenager knew it, the child did not)

This is fascinating, but I won't be troubled unless/until I find myself in a timeline that didn't have 9/11, the BP spill &/or Fukushima. THAT would be a strange experience to be sure!

So glad to have found you.

Kate says:

25 June 12 at 4:39 pm

This site is freaking me out. My friend Mikey and I used to talk about the Mandela memory all the time because we remembered him dying in prison. We used to talk about jumping time lines and we really believed it because things got 'different' for us both, but we NEVER talked about it with anyone else because of how insane it sounds! I have since then looked for anything about it, and I found this website- I just can't believe this. i also remember clearly the David Soule death—(i am shocked, up until I read this just now I still thought he was dead!) AND the Billy Graham death (Shocked) I do have one more for you, though. Donna Summer. The 80's disco singer? When she passed recently, I had a triple take to the tv–I have a very distinct memory of her dying in 2005–I was so upset because I used to love her voice–I remember it on the radio. I too, have had severely vivid 'dream occurances' and have always kept these to myself. I did once call George Noory on Coast to Coast to talk about it. I 'wake' up as another person in another timeline completely. (as if I go back to an earlier incarnation)The experience 'in there' seems to go on for a week or so...and the longer I am 'dreaming', the more THIS place seems like a dream and THAT place seems real. When I finally 'wake up' only twenty minutes have passed, and it takes me a day or two to shake the feeling and to realize that THIS is reality and my experience was the dream. Weird, huh? Anyway, I will certainly keep an eye in this website, thanks for making me feel a tiny bit less crazy about these things!

Paul says:
26 June 12 at 12:37 am

Well this is strange. I've often had issues with "false memory", but always pushed it aside because I figured "there's probably a logical explanation for this, I'm just too lazy to think of one." As for personal experiences, I have false memories that seem to be backed by physical evidence. The strangest one is that a few years ago a friend introduced me to the band Pendulum when he sent me one of their albums online, "Hold Your Colour". From that point, I always associated that band with the friend who got me to listen to them in the first place. About nine months later, the same friend heard me listening to their followup album "In Silico". He said "Oh, you like Pendulum too? Awesome." To which I replied "well yeah, you're the one that got me listening to them in the first place." And he said "What are you talking about? I've never heard of them until a couple weeks ago." None of my other friends listen to the band, and I'd never heard of them until nine months prior when this friend sent me the first album. In fact, it was one of the things that got us talking to each other more in the first place. He introduced me to the band, then we started sharing more music. I mean, I still have the album he sent me, but he had no recollection of sending it. He insists to this day that he had nothing to do with me liking Pendulum.

James says:

26 June 12 at 2:01 am

I remember distinctly watching an episode of Ed, Edd, 'n' Eddy which hadn't even appeared on the lineup during the day it was aired. It was the episode where the kids of the cul-de-sac discover that a quarter was stuck to the ground, and attempted every which way to remove it. I waited eagerly each following day waiting for the network to rerun that episode for some more of the good old laughs. Needless to say, I gave up on ever watching that episode again. It was only after 6 months, I saw the channel began to plug new episodes that were going to be aired in the coming weeks. That very episode aired on the block reserved for the new episode. I knew this because, at that time, the channel would overlay the words: "NEW EPISODE" just over the channel's icon overlay. I sat there, scratching my head, wondering what was happening and why they weren't showing a new episode that week, having already watched it. Never really thought anything of it.

Jacob Walse-Dominguez says:

31 May 13 at 1:01 pm

I remember that episode clearly! It was before the "new episodes" that they show these days! I'm confused, maybe they just re-branded episodes?

Brian says:

15 September 15 at 8:48 am

I had similar with an episode opening of the Simpsons: They beamed in. I have not *ever* found that opening again.

aragami says:

26 June 12 at 2:19 am

very interesting.

I remember robert stack dying in the 90's, ernest borgnine (sp?) being dead until i saw him in a new-ish movie, freddie prinze's baby, 52 states in the US, i always thought hondurus was an island, i saw the scene in star wars when i was a kid, and i very clearly remember the guy getting run over by the tank.

A couple of others – the movie 'survival quest'. I had this movie on vhs in the 80s, and watched it dozens of times. A couple of months ago i wastched it on sattelite tv, and it was completely different. The same actors, the same setting, the same general idea, but the almost every scene seemed to be from a seperate movie. I went so far as to check imdb and wiki, thinking there must be a sequal or something, and i had been confused as to which one i had on vhs. No sequal.

Personal story – i grew up on a huge farm with hundreds and hundreds of hereford (red) cattle. In one mob there were 3 huge old angus (black) cows that we called 'the hippos' due to their size and temperament. We all had running jokes about them, and always kept track of their calves, their calves calves and so on.

One day we were all sitting around talking about the new calves and i mentioned the hippos and how they always calved regularly. Everyone, mum, dad, my brother, our workmen, all stopped and looked at me. 'what are you talking about?'. We ended up arguing for half an hour. No-one had ever seen or heard of them. The next day i rode down the back to check, and couldn't find them. They were gone.

Josh says:
26 June 12 at 5:43 am

Wait, the guy didn't get run over by the tank?

miss_fionna says:

26 June 12 at 5:14 am

This is very strange to me.

I remember Mandela having died in prison. But I was very young then and I don't remember the exact event, but an anniversary of his death. It was all over the tv, they showed footage of him alive and some funeral footage too. Now I wasn't very old, but they were definitely talking about his death. I remember the so called "tank guy" being famous exactly because he was killed by that tank. (Again, this is a memory of a news event talking about it after the original event had occurred.)I also remember being taught that there was 52 states with Alaska being number 51 (even though at this point I only remember there being 50, and that was over ten years ago.

This discussion is really blowing my mind. I want to know what's going on.

Joseph says:

9 December 13 at 1:22 am

This freaked me out so badly when I heard that he didn't get run over. I had to do some research into this.

I remember it.

I remember watching it in school.

I remember his friends dragging his lifeless body away.

Apparently SEVERAL people remember him getting run over.

http://wiki.answers.com/Q/Did_the_Tank_Man_Tiananmen_
Square_get_run_over_by_a_tank&altQ=Who_was_tank_man_y
ou_tiananmen_square

Here is a link to a video that was supposed to show him getting run over, but the video is gone.

http://blog.fivefoldministryschool.com/wp-content/tmp/tiana
nmen-square-tank-man-run-over-video

But it gets even better.

Sooooo....

People remember the bloodshed right?

http://www.thenownewspaper.com/entertainment/musician-re
calls-the-bloodshed-of-china-s-tiananmen-square-1.512202

http://news.bbc.co.uk/2/hi/asia-pacific/3775463.stm

http://www.infowars.com/articles/ps/china_tourists_witness_bl
oodshed_tiananmen_square.htm

Well, apparently that didn't happen according to wikileaks.

http://www.telegraph.co.uk/news/worldnews/wikileaks/855514
2/Wikileaks-no-bloodshed-inside-Tiananmen-Square-cables-claim.
html

Here's a link to a blog covering the "Tianenmen Myth".

http://tiananmenmyth.blogspot.com/

Here's a link to the video as it is supposed to have happened.

Read the comments.

Reality gets freaking weirder every day.

Josh says:

26 June 12 at 5:42 am

Weird, I remember Billy Graham dying too....

To the people who remember being taught about 52 States, do you remember the names of the other two?

Also... just imagine... there's alternate timeline versions of this website too. You might come back to it one day and notice events mentioned on it have completely shifted.

David says:

15 June 13 at 7:21 pm

I am US History teacher in the US and my American students often mistakenly think there are 51 or 52 states at which I just shake my head and say,"kids today."

I think it's because there was a lot of talk about Puerto Rico becoming a state, which would have been the 51st... but it hasn't happened yet.

Getting back to Nelson Mandela I don't remember him dying but I do remember hearing about his wife becoming the leader of South Africa??? I think??? Was that in this timeline? or another?

Love this thread. Very interesting!!!!

Joseph says:

9 December 13 at 1:23 am

Here's the link to the video.

http://www.popscreen.com/v/6mMj3/Tank-Man-did-NOT-die -in-Tiananmen-Square

Kate says:

26 June 12 at 4:47 pm

On another website similar to this someone makes mention of something that happened in the mid 90's. A shift of some sort and that was when all these false memories started making their way to the surface. I don't know what to believe about anything anymore, but in the late 90's my friend and I talked about the same thing–about how something just 'changed' for us and it felt like we were not in the right 'spot' anymore. I know that's crazy, believe me I know how that sounds, but finding this site after everything my friend and I talked about so much during that time is kind of mind bending for me.

Brian says:

15 September 15 at 8:53 am

It happened to me in the early 90's. The jolt from what happened has left me in the state you are in. I just am unsure if it was a reality shift, or I got my butt kicked from one reality to another.

L. says:

26 June 12 at 7:12 pm

When I first read this article, I thought you meant that some people remember Billy Graham as being still alive. After I understood, I was shocked and had to double and triple check before fully believing it. I can clearly remember the death of Billy Graham and watching an interview of his widow talking about events from his life, his evangelism, how the two met, ect, with my grandma and talking about what a shame it was that such a good man died. I asked her if she remembered any of it, and was shocked when she told me that the only thing she could remember was his wife dying a few years ago. I thought she must be mistaken until I googled it. In my timeline I can remember channel surfing and her being on television with her son no longer than a year ago. The only reason I remember is because the Grahams live close to where I was born/grew up and at the time I thought it was cool that a local family was on television.

I also remember New Zealand being located to the northwest (odd, because most everyone who remembers an alternate position seems to recall it being to the northeast) of Australia and Australia being located further south and smaller. Also, I remember in school having to memorize and be tested on all the countries of North & South America. Honduras, Nicaragua, Costa Rica, and Guatemala were islands in relatively the same location; smaller and differently shaped but similar. Though its entirely possible I'm remembering that incorrectly as geography was never my forte.

As for personal experiences, I, my mother, and some of my immediate family remember my birthday as being the 27th of July. However, on my birth certificate, marked on old calendars/planners, my baby book, birthday cards, old party invitations kept for scrapbooks, ect, its listed as the 25th. I'm fairly certain I wouldn't forget my own birthday and always found it odd. Also, I remember my mother always saying 52 states instead of 50 when I was growing up and getting annoyed because she was a teacher and thats such common knowledge.

Someone mentioned that perhaps theres a connection between sliding and near death experiences. I was recently in the intensive care ward unconscious for a week and nearly died.

I'm glad I'm not the only one who has memories of Billy Grahams death, at least.

aragami says:

11 July 12 at 8:28 am

interesting you mention NDE's. I had a near death experience back in 2004 after a motorcycle accident.

nigel says:

13 July 13 at 2:19 am

I remember billy graham dying, nz being northwest of oz , but only 50 states, i do remember that terminator 2 scene and the star-wars one too...nelson mandela did die in prison in the 80s, jack palance, david soul, ernest borgnine all died along time ago too.

Hoss says:

26 June 12 at 8:32 pm

1. Alabama, 2. Alaska, 3. Arizona, 4. Arkansas 5. Colorado 6. California, 7. Connecticut, 8. Delaware, 9. Florida, 10. Georgia, 11. Hawaii, 12. Illinois, 13. Indiana, 14. Idaho, 15. Iowa, 16. Kentucky, 17. Kansas, 18. Louisiana, 19. Massachusetts, 20. Maryland, 21. Mississippi, 22. Maine, 23. Missouri, 24. Michigan 25. Minnesota, 26. Montana, 27. New Jersey, 28. New York, 29. North Carolina 30. New Hampshire, 31. Nevada, 32. Nebraska, 33. North Dakota

34. New Mexico, 35. Oklahoma, 36. Ohio, 37. Oregon, 38. Pennsylvania, 39. Puerto Rico. 40. Rhode Island 41. South Carolina, 42. South Dakota, 43. Tennessee, 44. Texas, 45. Utah, 46. Virginia, 47. Vermont, 48. Wisconsin, 49. West Virginia, 50. Washington, 51. Wyoming, 52. Washington DC

Some tv channel mistakenly reported that Billy Graham was dead: http://www.mediabistro.com/tvspy/wbtv-mistakenly-reports-death-of-billy-graham_b31294

Fiona Broome says:

27 June 12 at 5:59 am

Hoss, that's the list. Many people remember Puerto Rico finally achieving statehood, and — around the same time — D.C. became a state. So, that's 52.

That's pretty wild about the TV station making a mistake like that. I mean, it's not as if the staff would run with a major story without double-checking it, right...? And, they're referencing CBS News, which is the central office all the CBS affiliates get their information from. So, that makes this doubly strange. It sounds like someone in the news chain had a Mandela moment, and maybe more of them did.

Thanks for that link!

Cheerfully,

Fiona

5 July 12 at 2:04 am

My friend, who I often talked about this kind of thing with years ago, pointed out to mo tonight that Nelson Mandela and Billy Graham were born in the same year. Just some interesting serendipity. or is it? lol

C-Man says:

10 July 12 at 11:39 pm

WOW! this is really freaky!

Just around the last few months of last year, I had the sensation that something was 'different'. I was searching something on Google, and they created a sketch that celebrated Google's 12th birthday, which meant it was created in 1999, when I clearly remembering it being created in 2004. I also thought Mandela died in prison, and a couple of my friends share this memory. I also remember the Higgs boson being found back in 2006, when it just only recently was found. Plus, I remember the 2009 Star Trek movie coming out in 2003 instead. And I specifically remember there being 51 States, with Southern California becoming the 51st State. And apparently WW2 ended in 1945 instead of 1947. If anyone has any of these same memories, please reply. Thanks.

Frank says:

12 August 15 at 1:34 pm

I remember the tank running over the student too it was horrifying he was nothing but blood on the ground.

THE ORIGINAL MEMORIES LIST

T he following are *some* (not all) alternate memories that were discussed at the original Mandela Effect website, through 2019.

In most cases, they were reported by outliers and early adopters in Mandela Effect research *before* the topic started trending. That's why *this is one of the most reliable lists of genuine Mandela Effect memories.*

Most popular Mandela Effects

Berenstain Bears or Berenstein Bears - Which do you recall? (Still one of the most popular topics at this website.)

Billy Graham's funeral on TV, prior to his death on 21 Feb 2018.

Challenger shuttle explosion date? 1984, 1985, or 1986? Winter or another time of year? (Per Wikipedia, it was 28 Jan 1986.) Also, alternate memories about the *Columbia.*

Colors - Chartreuse and more - Many people recall chartreuse as a pink or reddish color. It's actually yellow-green.

Curious George - Tail or no tail? (He's never had a tail.) This is part of my article about dual memories.

***Ghost Hunters* TV show** - Some – including me – remember the earliest show name as *TAPS,* not *Ghost Hunters.* (Yes, we know the real-life team is called TAPS, and some of their gear has always said that.)

Henry VIII portrait with a turkey leg in his hand - Many people clearly recall seeing it in history books, but there's no record of it, now.

Jif or Jiffy Peanut Butter - Jif peanut butter was never called "Jiffy," in this timestream. (Not confused with Skippy brand, either.)

Lindbergh baby - Never found? In this timestream, the 20-month old baby *was* found 12 May 1932.

Mother Teresa - A saint before 2016? Several recall her canonization in the 1990s. They also recall her name spelled "Theresa."

Nelson Mandela's death in prison, long before his actual death (in this timestream) on 5 December 2013. (This was the alternate memory that launched MandelaEffect.com)

New Zealand's location, relative to Australia.

Red/blue - Pepsi logo changes, Chevron logo changes, and other color swaps... are they markers, cues, or signs to watch for?

September 22nd or 23rd? - Some people recall events shifting from one of these dates to another. (The reaction to this article - on- and off-site - has been disproportionate to its apparent minor importance.)

Sky - Changes in the sun, moon, stars, planets and their moons, constellation configurations and placement, and the color of the sky in general.

Tiananmen Square - Memories of a young man being run over by a tank. (Might be Mandela Effect issue or simple media manipulation.)

EVEN MORE MANDELA EFFECT EXAMPLES

More celebrities

Agatha Christie - Never found after her 1926 disappearance? (In this timestream, she turned up 10 days later, but never explained. Ref: http://en.wikipedia.org/wiki/Agatha_Christie#Disappearance)

Barbara or Barbra Streisand? In this reality, it's Barbra. ("Barbara" is a common typo, but doesn't explain all the alternate memories. Many people listed the alternative "Barbara" as one of several memories they have.)

Betty White - Alive, well, and still feisty at age 97 in July 2019, though some recalled her passing.

Brian Dennehy - Alive and well at age 80 (as of July 2019), per Wikipedia, but **a few of us have other memories**. And, I've seen 2019 reports of his death, as well. So, whatever is at work with Mandela Effect memories... this one seems persistent or at least recurring.

Charles Schulz or Schultz? (Creator of *Peanuts,* including Charlie Brown, Lucy, Snoopy, etc.) The correct spelling in this timestream is Schulz. (https://en.wikipedia.org/wiki/Charles_M._Schulz)

Charles Spencer, 9th Earl Spencer - Several people have (privately) reported a memory of his recent death. He's still alive and doing wonderful work for charities.

Coen brothers or Cohen brothers? - American film producers & screenwriters. *Note:* Different from producers John Cohen ("Ice Age," "Despicable Me," etc.), Rob Cohen ("The Mummy," "The Fast and the Furious," etc.), and Charles S. Cohen ("Frozen River.") Not the musicians, either.

David Soul - As of July 2019, he's still alive, healthy, and starring in new productions through 2020.

Dick Clark's death... at least two of them. (Per Wikipedia, he died in April 2012.)

Dick Van Patten - Died prior to his June 2015 death in this timestream?

Dom DeLuise's death. He died in 2009, but that's not the only memory people have.

Don Rickles - The sharp-tongued comedian passed away in April 2017 (per Wikipedia) although some recall his earlier demise... and some were sure he died much later in 2017. And, as of mid-2019, some people are sure they've seen him on TV - not pre-recorded - so they believe he's still alive.

Ernest Borgnine, death reported years before it happened in 2012.

Forrest J. Ackerman - Died in 2008 in this timeline (per Wikipedia), but others recall alternate, earlier death dates. He was certainly a man of mystery.

Fred Rogers (aka Mister Rogers) - Died in 2003, or later?

Freddie Prinze - Several memories, mostly related to **Freddie, Junior, and Sarah Michelle Gellar,** and a child born around 2003 or 2004.

Hal Holbrook - Born 1925, and still alive at age 94 in July 2019. His late wife, Dixie Carter, passed away in 2010. Several remember Mr. Holbrook's own death & memorials *prior* to 2010.

Helen Thomas (1920 - 2013), former White House reporter - Some recall an alternate date when she passed.

Henry Ford - Died from cerebral hemorrhage *or something else?*

Houston family (Whitney's) - Conflicting memories about her children, after Whitney's death, but before Bobbi Kristina's 2015 tragic death. Whitney's history seemed to stabilize after Bobbi Kristina passed; that's interesting. Are people (in this reality) a factor in how powerful/enduring some alternate memories are...?

Jack Palance - An earlier death date than what's in the current timestream.

Jayne Meadows Allen - Died 2015 or much earlier? (She was an actress, and widow of comedian Steve Allen.)

Jerry Lewis - Remembered death late in 2013 or early 2014. In this reality, he died in August 2017. Like the late Don Rickles, several people believe he died *much* later in 2017. (Different from Jerry Lee Lewis, the colorful singer/songwriter.)

Jim Henson - Died of complications from a strep infection, or from cancer? (In this timestream, initially reported as walking pneumonia. See https://en.wikipedia.org/wiki/Jim_Henson#Illness_and_death)

Jimmy Swaggart - Report dead, but still alive at age 84 in July 2019.

John Denver's death - When and where? In this reality, 12 Oct 1997 near Monterrey Bay, California.

John Lennon - Date of death is 8 Dec 1980, but some have clear memories of a different date.

John Lennon & Yoko Ono - The location of 1969 "bed-in for peace." (If you remember this, note the location *before* checking Wikipedia for the details.)

Jon Bon Jovi - Some recall a startling, mid-1990s lifestyle announcement.

Kathie Lee Gifford or Kathy Lee Gifford? In this reality, it's always been "Kathie."

Katy Perry - Memories of her using the name Kate, not Katy.

Leonard DiCaprio - Won an Oscar before 2016? Some recall earlier nominations and awards, as well as his 2016 acceptance speech, but years earlier.

Louie Anderson - Alive and well at age 66 in July 2019. Some recall his death (and, of course, end of his TV show) at some point in the past. (*Not* confused with John Candy and other comedians.)

Muhammad Ali - 2009 death? Died June 2016, per Wikipedia.

Neil Armstrong died in 2013, not 2012? Also, some are certain he made a 'Mr. Gorsky' reference during his lunar voyage. (Latter debunked in *this* timestream by Snopes, but does anyone actually recall *hearing* it?)

Patrick Swayze, his full recovery was reported *after* his tragic 2009 death in this reality.

Peter Fonda - He's still alive and well at age 79, as of July 2019. (Not confusing him with his dad, actor Henry Fonda, who died in 1982.)

Peter Townsend or Peter Townshend - Spelling change? (One is a singer-songwriter for The Who. The other is an American drummer.)

Reba McIntyre or Reba McEntire? - Decide how you remember it *before* visiting her official website or Wikipedia to see the real spelling.

Richard Chamberlain - Did *not* die in the 1990s. As of July 2019, he's 85. And - a related memory - James Franciscus was *not* his brother.

Robert Crumb - Death reported, 1990s. Still alive and irreverent at age 85, as of July 2019. Artist responsible for *Fritz the Cat* and the iconic *Keep on Truckin'* graphic, etc.

Robert Stack - Death reports before his actual passing in 2003. And, as of July 2019, some people report him still alive and appearing on TV.

Rod Serling or Rod Sterling? Some recall the latter spelling, not as a typo.

Rodney King - Some have alternate memories of his death, including one during the infamous incident in 1991.

Shirley Temple - Some recall her death long prior to 10 Feb 2014.

Sinbad - Did he ever play a genie in a major movie? Was it *Shazaam?* (And was it spelled *Shazam?*) Did he ever play a genie, full stop?

Terry Pratchett - According to some, he died shortly after the announcement of his illness (2013), instead of March 2015.

Will Smith and Jada Pinkett - Divorced ~10 years ago? (2019: Still listed as a happy couple and as romantic as ever. He divorced a previous wife in 1995.)

William Daniels (actor) - Did not die in the early 2000s. In fact, many recall him as Mr. Feeny in *Girl Meets World*, or the voice of K.I.T.T. in the *Lego Dimensions* game. Daniels is still witty and opinionated at age 92 (<- Wikipedia link) in July 2019.

Yogi Berra (athlete) - Died 22 Sep 2015, but some recall an earlier death.

More Mandela Effects... when and where?

9/11 - Did it happen on 9/11, as most people remember, or on 9/10, as some recall?

Thanksgiving (USA) - The third or the fourth Thursday in November? (Since 1941, it's always on the fourth Thursday.)

Weather - Hurricane Katrina: April or August 2005, or another year altogether?

Writers' strike in Hollywood - 2007-2008 or some other year (21st century only)? (This was long before the 2023 strike.)

More Mandela Effect geography

Geography - Locations and sizes of New Zealand. Locations of Australia, Honduras, Japan, Manchuria, and more.

Adam's Bridge (also Ram Setu, Rama Setu, *Setubandhanam*, and other names) - Some recall it fully above sea level in the mid-late 20th century, while historical records (in this timestream) say it was partially submerged - due to a cyclone - in the late 15th century. (ref: https://en.wikipedia.org/wiki/Adam%27s_Bridge)

51 or 52 United States - (Not Puerto Rico, which is a territory, or DC, which is a district.)

Alaska - Coastline radically different.

Arctica - Hasn't existed for a very long time.

Japan - Where do you recall it, in relation to China?

Korea - N. Korea borders Russia? That's what maps show.

Madagascar - Location and general geography. Not just a map issue.

Mongolia - Part of China or a separate country? And where is/was it?

Sri Lanka location, due south of India, not southeast.

Wales - East or west of England and Scotland? (It's west. From London, take the M25 west to the M4, and follow the M4 into Wales.)

More media memories (TV, films, books, magazines)

Big (the movie) - Alternate ending. (Not confused with *13 Going on 30.)*

The Candidate,* or *The Campaign - One movie, one and a remake, two movies, or now three... and did the title change? (Solved, maybe: See the related HuffPost page. Compare the article title and the inset video clip title.)

Carmen Sandiego ("Where in the World Is...") - Some recall a yellow trench coat, long before the red one.

Cinderella - Some recall an alternate central character or characters.

Cruella DeVille or De Vil? - It's the latter, in this Disney's *101 Dalmatians* movie reference.

Different Strokes or Diff'rent Strokes? - It's the latter, though many recall otherwise and some TV listings support that.

Duggars - Was the show (briefly) "21 Kids and Counting"?

Forrest Gump - Was the most famous line "Life IS like a box of chocolates..." or "Life WAS like a box of chocolates..."? In this reality, it's the latter. (However, *both* lines were used in connection with the movie, so this isn't necessarily a Mandela Effect.)

Fred Rogers' song, **"Won't You Be My Neighbor"** - Some recall "It's a beautiful day in *the* neighborhood." In this reality, it's "It's a beautiful day in *this* neighborhood." ? (See http://www.neighborhoodarchive.com/music/songs/wont_you_be_my_neighbor.html and https://youtu.be/zMUGJZrR9Jg .)

***Gremlins* character (movie) - Spike or Stripe?** The only reliable sources say it was *always* Stripe, not Spike. (But, as of November 2016, Gremlins has caved to popular memory. They actually licensed a t-shirt, calling the Gremlin "Spike.")

Hand gestures in movies - Do you recall *different* hand gestures in movies? For example, a more elaborate hand gesture by Antonio Banderas, with a candle, in **Interview with the Vampire**? See the YouTube clip from the movie, around the 2:03 point. I'm looking for very specific descriptions of the alternate gesture.

Independence Day (movie) - Characters now missing from a major scene? (This has been reported privately, twice, and we're looking for confirmation from others.)

Interview with *a* Vampire, or **Interview with *the* Vampire** - Actually, both titles were used on published book, in this reality. So, this isn't a clear Mandela Effect issue.

It's the Great Pumpkin, Charlie Brown, and related topics - Did the Great Pumpkin appear near the end of the holiday special, or was it just Snoopy's shadow? Was the cartoonist Charles Schultz or Charles Schulz? (In both cases, it was the latter in this reality.)

Jurassic Park - Original movie: Some recall a now-missing scene.

Justice League - Check the characters you're remembering and see if one is missing.

K-PAX (movie) - Starred Kevin Spacey or Nicholas Cage? (In this timestream, it's Spacey.)

Looney *Tunes* or Looney *Toons?* - Several conflicting memories.

Married with Children - Some recall one character played by two different actors.

M.A.S.H. (TV series) - Some recall the in-series death of Walter "Radar" O'Reilly. However, that wasn't part of the story in this timestream.

Mirror, Mirror - In "Snow White," did the evil queen say "Mirror, mirror..." or "Magic mirror..."? (In Disney's *Snow White and the Seven Dwarfs,* the Queen says, "Magic mirror.")

Mystery Science Theater - Variations of the numbers following show name (mostly 2000 or 3000, but a few recall 4000).

Sex and the City - Some are sure it was "Sex in the City" when it first aired.

Star Trek memories, including: Chakotay character killed, then returns - several episodes later - without much explanation. (I've talked about this - in person - with Robert Beltran, who played the character. He's *sure* that version was never written *or* filmed.)

Star Wars - Was the iconic line "Luke, I am your father" or "No, I am your father"? Also a missing scene. (Not just "deleted.")

Terminator (and other movie) variations, "remembered" *before* the deleted scenes were available on DVD. Alternate late scenes and endings reported, as well.

Who Framed Roger Rabbit? (movie) - Different ending after initial release? Different title?

X-Men - Some reports of alternate abilities for Professor X.

Movies remembered before they were released

Several movies have been "remembered" by people, months or years *before each movie was actually released.* When each person saw the film he or she reported, it was like *deja vu. Flushed Away* (2006) was the one most recalled as pre-2006.

More Mandela Effect-ish news reports

Twins... that aren't - Reports of people who look *exactly* like someone's twin (not just "somewhat like") but aren't actually twins. Different from doppelgangers, and more like the same physical design appearing again. Two alternates temporarily in the same reality...?

Whitey Bulger - Alleged Boston (MA, USA) gangster, died in 30 October 2018, *not* in 2013, in this reality. Much of his life - and weird ability to "hide in plain sight" - seemed laced with the Mandela Effect.

More politics and political leaders

Abraham Lincoln - Alternate death. Alternate death date of son, Tad, as well.

Fidel Castro - Died November 2016 (per Wikipedia), but some recall a 2011 death.

Martin Luther King, Jr. - Shot with a handgun, at close range, or another cause of death?

Muammar Gaddafi - Some death memories from years before he was killed (in this timestream), and a couple of memories of him fleeing his country.

Mussolini - Looks different in recent historical photos. Not just different photos from what are in older news articles and textbooks, but *a different man.*

Osama bin Laden - Death reported in 2001 in the Middle East and elsewhere, with obituaries. Actual death reported 2011. Apparent sightings since then could come from trolls.

Ronald Reagan - Varying memories about when he was president, and when and how he died.

More pop culture

Brian Williams' Southeast Asian memories - A high-profile example of Mandela Effect, a blunder, or something else?

Gaming - Alternate Versions...? Several reports related to different games, online and off.

Life cereal commercial (1970s) - **Did Mikey *like* everything, *eat* everything (or "eats anything"), or *hate* everything?** (In this reality, it was "he hates everything.")

Music - lyrics, tracks, videos, and more - that's a massive list, too long for this website.

Sara Lee products slogan/jingle - Some recall "Nobody *doesn't* *like* Sara Lee," (1960s' commercial: https://youtu.be/Iirw147LHkQ) but others recall it as "Nobody *does it* like Sara Lee." And, they're clear that they didn't just mis-hear it.

Volvo car symbol (the badge/icon/logo on the car)... Some recall a major change.

Spelling (names)

Berenstein - Berenstain (Bears books, etc.)
Dettol - Dettox (cleaning products)
Febreeze - Febreze
Fruit Loops - Froot Loops (breakfast cereal)

Jiffy - Jif (peanut butter)

Kathy Lee Gifford - Kathie Lee Gifford (entertainer)

Kate Perry - Katy Perry (entertainer)

Liason - Liaison

Looney Tunes or Looney Toons

MacDonald's - McDonald's (restaurant)

Oscar Meyer or Oscar Mayer? - Processed meat products' brand name.

Pete Townsend - Pete Townshend (drummer for The Who)

Reba McIntyre - Reba McEntire (entertainer)

Sketchers - Skechers (footwear brand name - It's Skechers in this reality.)

Western Sizzler - Western Sizzlin - Name in this timestream is Western Sizzlin (ref: https://en.wikipedia.org/wiki/Western_Sizzlin%27). Even FB pages lists Western Sizzler (ref: https://www.facebook.com/pages/Western-Sizzler-Auburn-Alabama/183908811678962).

(In every case, the latter spelling is correct in this reality.)

More spelling (dictionary)

Definitely or definately? Apparently, it's the most misspelled word in the English language, but where did "definately" come from and why do people remember being taught that spelling in school...?

Dilemma or dilemna? A *lot* of people seem to recall the latter (the version with an N), but - in this timestream - it looks like that was *never* the correct spelling.

Other *odd* topics

Disney theme parks

Disney World - Some people remember *entering* the Magic Kingdom through the castle. A second, alternate memory: Everything *else* matched the current timestream, but the castle was *much* closer to the end of Main Street. (At Disney World, not Disneyland.)

Disney World - Some people recall taking a monorail from the Orlando airport *directly* to the Disney World property. The Orlando airport has a train, not a monorail, and it doesn't take people to Disney World.

Disney World - A separate theme park in the Orlando (Florida) area. Maybe intended as a beta test site for attraction concepts? It's *not* an abandoned park or project, and it's much smaller (in acreage) than the main WDW property. Two main areas: (1) The theme park, and (2) one crescent-shaped building with shops and restaurants, plus one larger hotel on the other side of it. Generally, the theme park attractions are multi-level. (Note: *Not* confused with Universal Studios' theme parks.)

Mars - No moons or two moons?

Segway - Available in beta around 1996? (No. The company was started in 1999, and the product was in pre-production, limited release in 2002. Ref.)

MY MEMORY: MANDELA'S 20TH CENTURY FUNERAL

H ere's what I remember.

I saw it in the 1980s or early 1990s, and *thought* it was Nelson Mandela's funeral on the TV. (My family moved every few years, and my memories tend to have strong visual components. So, I connect the Mandela memory with where the TV was, and in which house. That's why I think my time frame is between 1985 and 1992.)

That day, I'd turned on the TV and the funeral had pre-empted all programming on all the major networks.

I remember the slow-moving vehicle with his casket revealed at the back of it.

I recall the huge crowds, with many weeping and wailing people, that lined the streets as the funeral vehicles passed.

The next day, I'd seen several televised speeches and tributes to Mandela's tremendous works, and his global legacy. One included a small – but well-secured – gathering of people in what looked like a rural setting.

I remember being impressed by the massive tree that towered over a simple podium, and the rows of folding chairs that faced it.

I vividly remember witnessing the emergence of Nelson Mandela's widow from a hidden spot situated just behind the colossal tree. She was dressed in black, and carrying a handkerchief she used to dab at her tears. She leaned heavily on the enormous bodyguard next to her, as she slowly – and somewhat unsteadily – made her way to the podium.

By the third (and final) day of coverage, I viewed just a few minutes of what was left of the tributes. I'd seen enough, and had other things to do.

I vaguely recall sporadic news coverage of rioting in South Africa, within days of the funeral. In my memory, those riots went on for two or three weeks, but – to be honest – in those days I didn't pay much attention to international news.

So, my clearest memories are related to the funeral that pre-empted TV shows that I wanted to see, and the really huge tree at the event where Mandela's widow spoke.

Later, realizing that Mandela was still alive, I decided that I must have been confused. The funeral had to be someone else's. However, I've never found any event that fit my memories.

If I ever do, I'm likely to laugh. Had it not been for that "mistaken memory," I might never have started the Mandela Effect website.

About the Author

In this book, I think most readers have a clear picture of who I am: A researcher with quirky interests, a dry (and sometimes zany) sense of humor, and someone *fascinated* by history and science.

Online, you may recognize me from what was – back in the 1990s – the largest, free, (and first) how-to ghost-related website, Hollow Hill.

(That name referenced Ireland's "hollow hills," since the site began as a history of the Tuatha De Danann legends and faerie lore. However, my ghost-related articles attracted the most attention, so the site's emphasis soon shifted. At its peak, that site was home to over 500 articles related to ghost hunting and haunted places.)

The Mandela Effect site was a fluke. I still look at the popularity of the phrase, and I'm astonished.

In real life, I've been a VIP guest and speaker at gatherings like Dragon Con, as well as lots of fun events at "haunted" sites from Texas to Maine, and Canada to England.

Other than that, I'm a very private person. Except for appearances on the History Channel, I've turned down all TV and most radio offers. And, though I've been portrayed in movies, no one contacted me for my permission, input, or feedback. (I explain this because, in general, some people seem to have a very odd view of me.)

However, if you see me at the grocery store, at church, or at the gym, it's okay to say hello.

You can find my articles and videos online, and my books are available through public libraries, bookstores, and – often, in early release – free through services like Amazon's Kindle Unlimited.

For my latest news, resources, freebies, and social media connections, visit my website, FionaBroome.com

Printed in Dunstable, United Kingdom